How to Cost Your
Labor Contract

How to Cost Your Labor Contract

Michael H. Granof

Department of Accounting
The University of Texas at Austin

**BNA
BOOK**

THE BUREAU OF NATIONAL AFFAIRS, INC. • WASHINGTON, D.C.

HD
4909
.G74
Cup. 2

Printed in the United States of America
Library of Congress Catalog Card Number: 73-77273
International Standard Book Number: 0-87179-191-9

Preface

The theme of this book is that collective bargaining is too important to be left to labor relations specialists. Labor costs are, for most firms, their single largest expenditure. As such, changes in outlays for employee compensation will necessarily have a substantial impact on functional areas of the firm other than labor relations. Decisions that are made at the bargaining table will influence the operations of the production department, the marketing department and the finance department. Collective bargaining is not an end in itself; it is a means of realizing the overall goals of the corporation. Contract proposals must therefore be analyzed within the context of the objectives, strategies and plans of the entire company, rather than within the more limited environment of the labor relations department.

The book is intended for labor relations managers. But, equally important, it is directed at accountants and finance managers as well. For they are the people who should be actively contributing to the collective bargaining process, but all too often are not.

This book is not a "how to do it" manual of contract analysis, even though it contains a number of practical examples of how to determine the cost of specific contract provisions. Such a manual would likely be of little value since problems facing individual firms are far too varied. Instead, the book proposes an approach to contract evaluation that requires explicit integration of plans relating to collective bargaining with those pertaining to other functional areas of the corporation.

Most of the research for this volume was done at the University of Michigan Graduate School of Business. James Bulloch, presently with the National Association of Accountants, worked closely with me, from the time the book was still an idea, in planning and conducting the research and in writing and editing the manuscript. Professors Meyer S. Ryder, John Stamm, James Arnold and C. Russell Hill, all of the University of Michigan, also read the various drafts and made helpful suggestions. Mr. Robert Gramen, of Arthur Andersen & Co., who was both an office mate and a neighbor while the book was written, served as a willing, though certainly nonvoluntary, sounding board for many of my ideas. Unfortunately, the many executives who gave many hours of their time cannot be thanked by name. I assured them that both they and their firms would remain anonymous.

Financial support for this research project was provided by the William Paton Fund of the University of Michigan and Ernst & Ernst.

M.H.G.
Austin, Texas

May, 1973

Table of Contents

TABLES

CHART

EXHIBIT

CHAPTER I

Introduction

Although the literature of both collective bargaining and accounting is rich, there is a dearth of published information on accounting as it relates to collective bargaining. Many corporate decisions relating to collective bargaining have considerable influence on corporate profits. Yet a manager faced with the task of predicting the most likely effect on revenues and expenses of a proposed labor contract could obtain but little guidance from the literature of either accounting or industrial relations.

The primary objective of this book is to provide direction to the executive who is charged with the responsibility of determining the financial consequences of labor contract proposals. The book will report and evaluate the means by which several major U. S. corporations cost out their labor contracts and will demonstrate how the discounted cash flow model—a technique widely used to evaluate and select from among alternative capital expenditure projects —can be employed to implement collective bargaining decisions.

Much of the information on widely used procedures to cost contracts was obtained from interviews with industrial relations, accounting and finance managers at 11 corporations. All of the firms are among the largest in their industries. Hence the methods they employ to evaluate contract proposals are likely to be typical of, though probably more sophisticated than, those of most of the others in their industries.

The first portion, the next three chapters, of this volume is devoted to a summary and evaluation of the practices of the firms interviewed. The second portion is given to a discussion of the discounted cash flow model.

Labor costs are, by far, the largest costs incurred by corporations. Each year, U. S. corporations spend over four times as much to compensate their employees as they do on new plant and equipment.

Because of the magnitude, the impact of labor costs on corporate profits is necessarily critical, and relatively small changes in either labor usage or compensation can result in relatively large changes in corporate profits. The means by which management can select the best labor contract package to contribute to the achievement of corporate goals are consequently worth consideration.

The essence of cost control is knowledge. In order to control expenditures for labor, management must know what those expenditures are and how they affect profits. When bargaining with unions, management must know—or be able to estimate—the effect on corporate profits of any proposed change in its labor contract before accepting or rejecting that change.

Insofar as management attempts to minimize increases in wages and benefits, its ability to control labor compensation is limited by its bargaining power vis-á-vis that of the union. Nevertheless, management can exert considerable influence on labor costs. For the cost of labor depends not only on the overall size of the compensation package, but on its component parts as well. A union might well be indifferent as between two alternative contract changes; the two might have identical utility to its members. Yet the effect on corporate profits of the two alternatives might be entirely different. To the extent that management is free to select between the alternatives, it can exercise an important control function over labor costs.

Evaluation of the financial implications of changes in labor contracts is especially important; the costs of poor decisions are likely to be high. Mistakes made during collective bargaining are not easily rectified. Many contracts are for three-year periods, so it may be almost that long before specific contract clauses are even open to negotiation. But, in addition, benefits granted for the duration of a contract may become permanent benefits if a union is able to exact a sufficiently high price when management wants to rescind a benefit to which employees have grown accustomed. Should a company overestimate the influence on profits of a wage package, it might take a costly, though unnecessary, strike rather than accept union demands. Should it underestimate the effect on profits, it might be unable to compete successfully with firms in its industry which did not sign a similar contract.

The task of evaluating the financial impact of contract proposals is formidable. First, the financial burden of "fringe benefits" (compensation in addition to direct hourly wages) is especially difficult to estimate. Fringe benefits are a part of virtually all labor contracts, and the number of workers receiving a variety of benefits is rapidly increasing. Second, contract clauses which do not directly involve compensation, such as those dealing with work schedules, job classifications, seniority rules and training programs, are not easily quantified yet have a significant financial impact. Third, and perhaps most important, the relationships between labor costs and other aspects of a firm's operations are often elusive. For example, changes in volume, product mix, and capital investment are likely to influence the amount of labor used. But changes in the amount of labor may in turn affect the firm's volume, product mix, and capital investment.

Although corporations exert considerable effort in determining the costs of proposed changes in their labor contracts—many compute costs to four decimal places—the evidence suggests that such effort is often misdirected.

TABLE 1.1

APPROXIMATE ADDITIONAL COST OF UNION DEMANDS
AS COMPUTED BY A "TYPICAL" COMPANY

Union Proposals	Shop	Office	Total
20¢ general increase (nonincentive workers)			
80 shop employees—			
80 x 2,080 = 166,400 x 20¢	$32,512.00		
64 office employees—			
64 x 2,080 = 133,120 x 20¢		$26,624.00	$59,136.00
3 wks. vacation after 10 yrs. (presently 2 wks.) @ av. hrly. earnings			
Shop 58 employees—			
58 x 40 @ $2.14	4,964.80		
Office 24 employees—			
24 x 40 @ $1.72		1,651.20	6,616.00

TABLE 1.1—Contd.

Union Proposals	Shop	Office	Total
Holidays—2 extra @ av. hrly. earnings			
Shop 110 employees—			
110 x 16 @ $2.14	3,766.40		
Office 64 employees—			
64 x 16 @ $1.72		1,761.28	5,527.68
Holidays falling on Saturday— 2 @ av. hrly. earnings			
Shop 110 employees—			
110 x 16 @ $2.14	3,766.40		
Office 64 employees—			
64 x 16 @ $1.72		1,761.28	5,527.68
Rest periods—Two 15 min. periods @ av. hrly. earnings			
Shop 110 employees—			
110 x 245 days worked			
110 x 245 x .5 x $2.14	28,836.50		28,836.50
Office already has rest periods			
Furlough employees—group insurance coverage @ 5¢ per hr.			
10 shop employees—			
2,080 hrs. x .05	1,040.00		
5 office employees—			
2,080 hrs. x .05		520.00	1,560.00
Tool grinders—15¢ increase in add. to gen. inc.			
2 employees—2 x 2,080 x .15	624.00		624.00
Machine operators (30 not included in gen. inc.)			
(a) $2 base rate plus 1/6 prem. + 20¢ (min.)			
(b) $2 base rate plus 30% prem. + 20¢ (max.)			
(a) 1/6 or 16.6% of $2 = .333¢ + 20¢ = 53¢ min.			
(b) 30% of $2 = 60¢ + 20¢ = 80¢ max.			
$.80 + .53 = \dfrac{1.33}{2} =$			
.66 av. hrly. increase			
30 employees working and paid for 2,080 hrs. x .66	38,808.00		38,808.00

TABLE 1.1—Contd.

Union Proposals	Shop	Office	Total
Jury duty pay differential (approx. $9 day)			
Av. 8 employees year 14 days	1,008.00		
Av. 2 employees year 14 days		252.00	1,260.00
Bereavement pay min. 3 days @ av. hrly. earnings			
Av. 10 shop employees year 3 days	513.60		
Av. 2 office employees year 3 days		72.64	586.24
Wash-up time nonincentive workers 10 min. day			
80 shop employees—245 days worked—10 min. x av. hrly. earnings			
$\frac{80 \times 245 \times 10}{60} =$			
3,266 hrs. @ $2.14	6,989.24		6,989.24
Total Additional Costs			155,471.34

Source: National Industrial Conference Board, PREPARING FOR COLLECTIVE BARGAINING, Studies in Personnel Policy No. 172 (New York: National Industrial Conference Board, 1959), p. 103.

Table 1.1 illustrates how a typical company might compute the cost of its union's demands. Commonly the costs of union demands are expressed in four ways:[1]

1. *Annual cost.* This is the total sum expended by the company over a year on a given benefit; usually the sum excludes administrative costs. Most companies make computations similar to those illustrated to arrive at the annual cost of a benefit.

2. *Cost per employee per year.* This is determined by dividing the total cost of a benefit by either the average number of employees for the year or the number of employees covered by a particular program.

---

[1] National Industrial Conference Board, COMPUTING THE COST OF FRINGE BENEFITS, Studies in Personnel Policy No. 128 (New York: National Industrial Conference Board, 1952), p. 7.

3. *Percent of payroll.* This is the total cost of the benefit divided by the total payroll. Most companies include in total payroll all payments to all employees, but some exclude overtime or shift-differential premium pay.

4. *Cents per hour.* This is derived by dividing total cost of the benefit by total productive hours worked by all employees during the year.

All four expressions suffer in common from one major defect: They have little relevance for corporate decision-making. They can provide only the most general, and possibly misleading, guidance for labor negotiators. The weaknesses of these expressions result from these oversights: (1) They fail to take into account how a firm will adapt to the new labor contract. (2) They ignore opportunity costs. (3) They ignore both cash flow and the time value of money.

(1) The expressions fail to take into account how a firm will adapt to the new labor contract; they are static rather than dynamic. A change in labor costs cannot be viewed in isolation from other decisions a firm must make. One should not say, "all other things held constant, the cost of the benefit will be X dollars." All other things will not, or certainly should not, remain constant. For example, if a firm produces more than one product, it is unlikely that the ratio of labor costs to total costs is the same for each of the products. Insofar as an increase in wage rates makes the labor-intense products less profitable relative to the other products, the firm might decrease production of the labor-intense products and increase production of the others. Once the product mix is changed, it is clear that the overall effect on profits should not be computed merely by multiplying hours worked in the previous year (or even hours expected to be worked in future years ignoring the wage increase) by the increase in wages.

Many firms attempt to raise prices in the period immediately following agreement on a new labor contract. If customers accept the higher prices (that is, demand is relatively inelastic), then total revenue of the firm will increase. But if they resist the higher prices, sales decline, and eventually the firm has to reduce production. Any computation of the financial impact of a new contract that fails to consider the changes in production and revenue fails to indicate the true consequences of the new contract on profits.

An increase in wage rates should induce a firm to review not only its product mix and prices, but also its use of factors of production. To the extent that the firm had previously been operating with the optimum proportion of labor to capital, the new contract might prompt the firm to increase the use of capital relative to labor. As an illustration, if a firm uses discounted cash flow techniques to evaluate investment proposals, then the present value of the incremental cash flows associated with labor-saving equipment would increase. Presumably, projects which were previously near the margin of acceptance would now be undertaken when reevaluated in the light of the increased labor costs (assuming, of course, that the cost of the project is likely to remain constant). Insofar as the increased use of capital reduces the use of labor, it is again clear that the "static" approach of estimating the cost of a labor contract fails to consider the overall financial consequences of the contract and is, therefore, of limited usefulness in making bargaining decisions.

Among other decisions that must be reviewed in terms of a new labor contract are those involving depth of processing, adoption of new products, abandonment of old products and continuation of operations at a loss. To ignore the possibility of revising previously formulated plans is to overlook management's ability to adjust to changing conditions.

(2) The expressions of cost ignore the costs of lost opportunities. The computation of the cost of rest periods as illustrated in Table 1.1 is a case in point. The cost of rest periods was computed by multiplying number of minutes of additional rest time by number of employees by number of days worked by average hourly wage rate. But what if the firm is already operating at capacity? The wages of the employees will be unaffected by the increase in rest time. The employees will work the same number of hours each day, but they may produce less. The cost to the firm cannot be measured in terms of wages paid to the workers while they are not productive. Since employees would be unable to recoup lost production by working overtime, the firm may lose sales, and presumably profits, because of the reduced production. Thus, the true cost is the variable profit on the lost sales, not the "increase" in wages.

(3) The costs of contract benefits as traditionally computed

ignore both cash flow and the time value of money. Since many contracts extend over a three-year period, and since the cost of capital for many companies is over 10 percent per year, the time value of money is not trivial in calculating labor costs. A benefit granted for only the third year of a contract is, therefore, far less costly than a similar one granted for only the first year. Comparisons among alternative proposals are difficult unless they are stated in common (present value) dollar terms.

The "traditional" expressions of cost (annual cost, cost per employee per year, percent of payroll and cents per hour) could easily mislead management into selecting the more costly of two alternative contract proposals. But they might also permit managers to delegate to unions authority to make decisions which should properly be made jointly by labor and management. One experienced negotiator, for instance, reports that it is common practice when labor and management are near an agreement for management to offer a wage increase stated in terms of cents per hour and to allow the union to distribute the increase among any of several benefits. Unless the amounts involved are trivial, management may be yielding important control over labor costs, for it is unlikely that the cents-per-hour expression is indicative of the true effect on profits.

Although both academicians and practitioners have demonstrated the applicability of quantitative techniques such as mathematical modeling and computer simulation to decision-making in regard to production, capital budgeting and marketing, few attempts have been made to apply these techniques to collective bargaining. One researcher surveyed 225 firms listed in the FORTUNE DIRECTORY to assess the use of computers in collective bargaining. Only seven companies reported that they used specially designed computer programs to estimate the cost of anticipated union demands, and only one company reported that it had developed a mathematical model to assist in making projections of relevant variables. Not a single company reported that it used, on an ongoing basis during negotiations, mathematical models or simulations to test the effects of alternative demand packages. The use of quantitative techniques such as mathematical modeling or simulation cannot, of course, be equated with the use of computers, but because of the great number of computations often required by such techniques, the correlation between the two is likely to be high. The researcher found that the most common use of the computer was to produce routine reports similar to those prepared by conventional methods. He concluded that "the use of computers to prepare for bargaining is in its infancy—or possibly it is still in the foetal stage." [2]

New approaches to the determination of the financial impact of proposed labor contracts are needed. One possibility might involve the application to labor contracts of techniques used to evaluate long-term capital projects. Specifically, the discounted cash flow model, a capital budgeting model that has received acceptance among both accounting theoreticians and corporate managers, might be used to evaluate alternative labor contract proposals.

The discounted cash flow model requires its user to estimate the incremental cash flows that would result from accepting each capital project under consideration. Using an appropriate "cost of capital," or "internal rate of return" expressed as a percentage rate, the expected cash flows over the life of the projects are "discounted" back to the present—i.e., the present value of the sums of the cash flows are computed. The projects are then ranked according to the magnitude of their net cash flows.

One of the primary advantages of the discounted cash flow model in making investment decisions is that it requires a manager to estimate explicitly the incremental cash flows that can be expected over the life of the project. He must consider not only the direct receipts and disbursements associated with the project, but cash flows in all aspects of the firm's operations that would be affected if the project were to be accepted.

Were a manager to use such a model to evaluate alternative labor contract proposals, he would similarly have to take into account both direct and indirect changes in cash flows attributable to the new contract. He would have to recognize explicitly changes in price, volume, product mix and labor-capital mix, as well as any others that the firm might make in its attempt to adjust to the

2 William G. Caples, *The Computer's Uses and Potential in Bargaining: A Management View*, in Abraham J. Siegel (ed.), THE IMPACT OF COMPUTERS ON COLLECTIVE BARGAINING (Cambridge, Mass.: The MIT Press, 1969), p. 79.

new contract—changes which he would not specifically recognize if he used the traditional cost-oriented methods. The opportunity cost of revenue lost owing to reduced volume would automatically be taken into account and so, too, would the time value of money.

CHAPTER II

Environment for Financial Analysis

In this chapter, and in the following two, the means by which corporations evaluate contract proposals will be reviewed. This chapter will be concerned with the departments which have responsibility for formulating bargaining strategy and analyzing contract proposals. It will also explore the timing of preparations, the types of data used, and the role of computers in contract evaluation. The following two chapters will deal with specific procedures employed to assess the financial ramifications of contract change.

All of the corporations at which interviews were conducted were among the *Fortune* 500" or equivalent, and nine of the 11 were among the largest 100 of the *Fortune* 500" or equivalent.[1] A variety of industries were represented in the study:

Aerospace	Glass
Airlines	Meatpacking
Autos	Oil
Auto supplies	Rubber
Chemicals	Steel
Drugs	

Sales of the companies studied ranged from $270 million to several billion dollars. Assets ranged from $400 million to almost $10 billion.

In all firms, labor costs were substantial and the number of persons employed by the firms ranged from 14,000 to over 400,000.

---

[1] THE FORTUNE DIRECTORY, May 1970. The airline visited is included among the 50 largest transportation companies.

Appendix I contains additional information on the methodology of the study.

RESPONSIBILITY FOR COLLECTIVE BARGAINING

In each of the companies studied, primary responsibility for collective bargaining is vested in an industrial or labor relations department. Non-industrial-relations personnel, such as accountants, financial analysts or members of top management, however, exert varying degrees of influence on bargaining decisions.

In several companies, accounting or finance officers are members of the bargaining team. Among the positions they hold are: vice president, treasurer and controller; assistant treasurer; accountant; financial analyst. A vice president who was interviewed suggested that his function during negotiations is a relatively passive, albeit essential, one. He serves primarily as a "lookout" for contract terms which might prove especially troublesome in ways of which the labor relations staff might be unaware. He cited an example of why he believes it important for the financial function to be represented at the bargaining table:

> At a recent bargaining session, the union asked that the company withhold union dues from its members in varying amounts based on the average hourly wages of the employees rather than in fixed amounts as was the current practice. The industrial relations personnel were ready to accede to the request; it would apparently cost the company nothing. But the financial officer pointed out that the company's accounting system would be unable to provide the average hourly earnings data when needed without major—and costly—revision.

Seldom do accounting or finance personnel assist in formulating bargaining strategy (e.g., determining at what point in the negotiations various offers should be presented and deciding what information, in addition to that required by law, should be given to union negotiators). That function is within the province of industrial relations personnel.

In all companies studied, top-level management (e.g., the president, an executive committee, the general managers of corporate divisions) have ultimate authority to accept or reject proposed settlements. As indicated in Table 2.1, the extent to which top management actually exercises its authority, however, differs from firm to firm. In one company, an executive committee, composed of the president, corporate controller, vice president of finance, vice president and treasurer, and the vice presidents of the major operating divisions, reviews all contract proposals before they are presented to the union. During negotiations the committee advises the bargaining team as the talks progress and approves or rejects any settlement proposal. In another company, however, top management exercises *de jure* but not *de facto* authority over proposed settlements. The president, chairman of the board, and vice president of personnel establish guidelines for the new contract, but once they do so they remove themselves from the bargaining process and delegate responsibility for achieving a settlement to the director of industrial relations. The director of industrial relations stressed that "the 'front office' never approves a specific contract."

TABLE 2.1

SUMMARY OF ROLES OF "TOP" MANAGEMENT IN
COLLECTIVE BARGAINING [1]

No. of Firms	Role
3	Plays inactive role; establishes broad guidelines but does not get involved in negotiations.
6	Plays moderately active role; establishes guidelines; "stands by" during negotiations to make policy decisions; approves or rejects proposed settlements, but generally accepts recommendation of chief negotiator.
2	Plays active role; establishes guidelines; is consulted on all significant issues raised at bargaining table.

[1] "Top" management includes the president, executive vice presidents, members of an executive committee, and general managers of divisions.

More commonly, top operating executives establish guidelines, are kept informed of the progress of negotiations and give formal approval to settlements when recommended by the officer in charge of negotiations. In their study, MANAGEMENT PREPARATION FOR COLLECTIVE BARGAINING, Ryder, Rehmus and Cohen found that "central administrative officers within the corporation, especially the president, hold the ultimate decision-making authority," but that in many cases "the corporation presidents exercise their authority only in a *pro forma* sense, since the real decisions have already been made." [2] They noted that the actual decisions tend to be made by executive or industrial relations committees or personnel or industrial relations executives. The findings of the present study are in accord with those of Ryder, Rehmus and Cohen.

DEPARTMENTS WHICH SUPPLY AND ANALYZE DATA

In almost all companies, the accounting and/or finance departments supply data, upon request, to the industrial relations department. But few other generalizations can be made with regard to the nature or scope of the data supplied. In some companies the accounting or finance departments do nothing more than provide the industrial relations department, upon request, with data taken directly from payroll records. In others they work closely with the industrial relations department and supply skilled personnel as well as data. But in only a very few companies do the finance or accounting departments have primary responsibility for performing financial analyses of contract proposals. Most frequently, as indicated in Table 2.2, such responsibility rests with the industrial relations department.

TABLE 2.2

SUMMARY OF DEPARTMENTS WHICH ANALYZE FINANCIAL
IMPACT OF CONTRACT CHANGES

No. of Firms	Department
5	Primarily Industrial Relations
1	Primarily Compensation
2	Industrial Relations and Accounting
1	Primarily Accounting
2	Primarily Finance

In one of the smaller companies, the director of industrial relations does virtually all cost analysis (except that of insurance and pension benefits) himself. The accounting department provides

---

[2] Meyer S. Ryder, Charles M. Rehmus and Sanford Cohen, MANAGEMENT PREPARATION FOR COLLECTIVE BARGAINING (Homewood, Ill.: Dow Jones-Irwin, 1966), p. 43.

payroll data when it is requested (which the director of industrial relations indicated is seldom), but otherwise remains uninvolved with collective bargaining. The director of industrial relations does not obtain and does not seek—except to the extent that he reads the corporate annual reports—information regarding the company's financial condition or plans for the future. He agreed that additional accounting and financial information might enable him to make a more comprehensive analysis of contract proposals, but he thought that if he established closer relations with the accounting or finance department he would compromise the security of management's strategy by permitting those outside the industrial relations department to be aware of what proposals management was seriously considering. Surprisingly, the accounting department does, in fact, cost out new contracts, but only *after* they have been signed. The purpose of the after-the-fact review is to make certain that the computations of the industrial relations department are sufficiently reliable to be used in corporate profit plans.[3]

A company in which the finance department has primary responsibility for determining the effect on profits of proposed contract changes appears to devote far more man-hours to preparation for negotiations than do other firms studied. In the weeks preceding the opening bargaining sessions at least 10 persons from the finance department are assigned to contract analysis. Consequently, the firm's projections are far more detailed than those of the other firms. The industrial relations department confines itself to examining and evaluating "nonfinancial" aspects of contract proposals, but the working relationship between the industrial relations department and the finance department is close.

More typical, however, is the firm in which the accounting or finance department and the industrial relations department share in the financial analysis of contract changes. In one manufacturing firm, for example, the accounting department furnishes the industrial relations department with "bargaining statistics," which are essentially information on the historical cost of particular items of

---

[3] When told of this company's policy of maintaining security of strategy by confining all analysis to the industrial relations department, an executive of another company indicated that his firm takes a different approach to protecting its plans. It informs the union that all contract proposals—no matter how absurd they may seem—will be analyzed and the fact that a proposal is being examined is no indication that it is being given serious consideration.

compensation summarized in a form useful to the industrial relations department. If the industrial relations department wants to compute the costs of proposed contract changes it either does so itself, based on data already provided by the accounting department, or requests additional assistance or data from the accounting department.

In a divisionalized company there may be special problems of providing necessary information to decision-makers if payroll records are maintained by the accounting departments at the divisional level and negotiations are conducted by the industrial relations department at the corporate level. The industrial relations department may have to deal with intermediaries in order to obtain the information it requires. In one company, for example, a master agreement is negotiated by the corporate industrial relations department and there is no communication between the industrial relations department and the divisional accounting departments. Instead, the corporate industrial relations department requests data from the divisional industrial relations departments which in turn request them from the divisional accounting departments. Perhaps because of the difficulty of obtaining detailed information, the director of industrial relations receives only the most general types of cost information, usually on a single typewritten page or over the telephone. But divisionalization need not be a barrier to effective communication. In another divisionalized company, a corporate compensation department is responsible for collecting and analyzing much of the payroll and financial data used by the industrial relations department. The compensation department serves as a liaison between the corporate industrial relations department and the divisional accounting departments and provides whatever cost estimates are requested by the corporate industrial relations department. More than by coincidence, the accounting data supplied to the industrial relations department in this company are far more detailed than those given to the industrial relations department of the first firm, and, perhaps as a result, the cost analyses are considerably more comprehensive.

All companies visited have pension and insurance specialists on their staff. Although sometimes assigned to a benefits or compensation department, they work closely with the industrial relations department, and often are members of the bargaining team.

RELATIONSHIPS AMONG DEPARTMENTS

In some companies, formal lines of communication have been established for transmitting information between the industrial relations department and the accounting and finance departments. In others, information is exchanged through informal, and often haphazard, contacts among departments.

Whereas some industrial relations managers automatically receive periodic reports from the accounting or finance departments, others receive specific data only upon request. Not surprisingly, the managers who automatically receive periodic reports minimized the importance of informal channels of communication; those who do not, emphasized it.

One industrial relations director who does not receive formal reports indicated that in evaluating contract proposals he very definitely takes into account both anticipated sales volume and the ability of the firm to pass on to customers, in the form of higher prices, any increases in labor costs. But he obtains estimates of sales volume and price increases by periodically having lunch with plant managers and "over a martini" obtaining a "feel" for corporate prospects.

Some industrial relations officers would not trust formal reports even if they did receive them. One industrial relations director, in a company whose corporate planning department prepares comprehensive and highly sophisticated profit projections, appraises the financial burden of contract changes using forecasts of future volume made by his own department. He commented: "Our estimates are as good as theirs." By contrast, those managers who periodically receive copies of corporate profit and sales forecasts and other reports dealing with corporate plans, indicated that they are willing to rely upon the estimates contained in the reports as the foundations of their own cost estimates. Information obtained informally, they said, was superfluous.

Industrial relations officers often tend to view the accounting and finance departments as performing a staff function for their own departments. That is, their departments request analyses and information; the accounting and finance departments provide them. A noteworthy exception, however, is an industrial relations manager of a company in which the finance department has primary responsibility for the cost analysis of contract proposals. In his company, the manager emphasized, the industrial relations department does not specifically solicit information from the finance department; instead it is the *function* of the finance department to supply such information. It does so as a matter of routine rather than request. If the industrial relations department and the finance department should disagree as to assumptions underlying the computation of the cost of a contract change, the dispute would be referred to the vice president of finance, rather than to an industrial relations executive, for settlement.

In general, it appears that more formal ties contribute to a more frequent exchange of information among departments. And the contributions of accountants and finance specialists tend to make for a more complete review of contract proposals.

TIMING OF PREPARATIONS

When industrial relations executives are asked when preparations for forthcoming negotiations begin, they invariably reply, "The day after the current agreement is signed." In fact, however, most firms begin to cost out contracts changes anywhere from two months to a year before the expiration of a contract. Often the timing of preparation is governed either by negotiations in related industries or by various union activities. A company whose employees are represented by the United Automobile Workers, for example, does not begin to cost out anticipated proposals until the union has presented its demands to one of the Big Three auto companies. The company begins to gather general economic data and information about wage settlements in related industries about a year in advance of the expiration of its contract. Several months before expiration it prepares position papers on various anticipated union demands, but it does not compute specific dollar costs until two or three months before negotiations are scheduled to begin. By that time the union has usually settled with one of the Big Three, and the demands of the union are quite clear.

Similarly, a major oil company begins its cost analysis shortly after the union with which it bargains holds its national convention—about 10 months preceding the start of negotiations at a major plant. About six months before the talks commence, union officials meet again to formulate "mandatory demands." As soon as these are known to the company, it is able to begin detailed cost analysis.

One manager indicated that his firm does not cost out a specific contract proposal until the union has actually placed it on the table. The company, a multi-division corporation that engages in plant-level negotiations, starts its preparation about six months before talks begin. During those six months the industrial relations department attempts to identify sections of the contract that have been troublesome to management. Most such sections involve "non-economic" issues such as work rules or ambiguous contract language. The bargaining team meets periodically to develop negotiating strategy and management establishes guidelines for the overall cost of the settlement it will be willing to accept. The manager pointed out that, although he is concerned with the components of the contract to the extent particular benefits "do not get out of line," he concentrates his attention on the total cost of the package. Hence, he is much more willing than officials of many other companies to allow the union to distribute the increase over the various components as it sees fit, and he is willing to wait until he receives the union demands before determining their specific cost.

SEQUENCE OF BARGAINING DECISIONS

In all companies, consideration is given to overall cost relatively early in the process of evaluating a proposed contract. Most prevalently the overall cost of a contract is the starting point for the development of the company's proposals. Once the total cost is established, the company decides among which of the components the increase is to be distributed. Sometimes, however, the total cost of the contract is variable. Increases in particular benefits are considered concurrently with the total increase the company is willing to grant and the total contract cost is strongly influenced by the costs of particular benefits. Typical is the process in which top management, often an executive committee, establishes guidelines for a settlement and the industrial relations department is allowed to vary the components of the contract within those guidelines. Total contract cost is one of the major restrictions established by top management, but it is usually not the only one. Some union

demands involve matters of principle and management will not permit negotiators to accede to them regardless of cost. One negotiator, for example, stated that he is prohibited from even discussing
a cost of living increase with his union counterparts.

Several managers interviewed acknowledged that their firms
seldom initiate contract changes on their own. Instead, they respond
to demands of the unions. One company, for example, first examines
the demands of labor and estimates their cost. Top management
determines the maximum amount that the company can "afford,"
and the industrial relations staff develops proposals that it believes
will best satisfy the union within the guidelines that have been
established.

A number of industrial relations executives pointed out the
importance of evaluating the components of a contract as well as
its overall cost. They noted that they would by no means be indifferent among all increases of equal cost. One executive explained
that if his company were to allow one benefit to increase relative
to industry standards and another to decrease, it would, when the
next contract was negotiated, have to grant an extraordinarily large
increase in the lagging benefit. For example, should the company
grant an unusually generous pension plan in exchange for a parsi-
monious health insurance plan, the union at the next negotiating
session would likely demand that the company increase its health
insurance plan to a level comparable to those of other firms in its
industry. But it would not, of course, accept a reduction in the
benefits already won. Another executive explained that his firm generally attempts to increase wages at the expense of benefits. His firm
is in competition with many small, often nonunionized companies
that are much more likely to follow the lead of his company—and
thereby increase their costs—in offering direct wage raises than they
are in granting benefit increases.

DATA USED TO EVALUATE THE FINANCIAL IMPACT OF ALTERNATIVE CONTRACT PROPOSALS

Companies can be divided by type of data used to evaluate
contract proposals into three groups:
1. those that use primarily demographic data but make little
   use of either accounting or other financial data;

2. those that use primarily demographic and accounting data, but make little use of other financial data; and

3. those that use all three types of data.

The term "demographic data" is used herein to describe the "vital" statistics of an employee population, e.g., number of employees and distribution of ages, sexes, number of dependents, rates of pay and years of service. "Accounting data" is used to describe information that can usually be obtained from payroll records, e.g., amounts paid in direct wages, overtime premiums, military leave pay, vacation pay, and holiday pay. "Other financial data" is used to describe internal economic data that are not directly related to payroll costs. It would include information, such as past, or estimated future, revenues, production volume, product mix, and nonlabor costs, that is normally found in a corporate budget or profit report.

Firms that use primarily demographic data but make little use of accounting or financial data. Industrial relations officers of each of the firms (three of 11) that use primarily demographic data indicated that, except to the extent that they usually attempt to negotiate a contract with the lowest direct dollar or cents-per-hour cost, they give no consideration to the impact of the contract on the profits of the firm. They emphasized the view that bargaining is a "subjective" process, and they minimized the importance of accurate estimates of costs. Instead, they stressed the importance of general economic data, information on settlements reached by other companies in their own or related industries and their assessments of employee attitudes, as opposed to internal accounting information. "We keep profits in mind," commented the director of labor relations of an oil company, but they are not the paramount consideration.

All of these companies do, of course, estimate the costs of contract changes, but they do so in a manner that requires the use of little or no accounting data. That is, they do not take into account the historical behavior of labor costs. They do not consider, for example, the amount of overtime worked, the number of workers who receive additional pay in lieu of vacation time off, or the actual amounts paid for time not worked. They might, therefore, compute the cost of an additional holiday by simply multiplying the number of employees times the number of work hours in a day times the average hourly rate of pay—regardless of the number of men who usually work on a holiday, the amount of production that will be lost because of the holiday and the manner in which the lost production will be recovered.

In the companies visited, demographic data are obtained by the departments in charge of contract analysis from a variety of sources. Often, such data are supplied by a personnel or compensation department. Less frequently, they are supplied by a payroll or treasury department. In every company, demographic data are given by the industrial relations department both to insurance companies and actuarial consulting firms and to pension and insurance experts within the firm who actually perform the cost analyses of pension and insurance provisions.

Firms that use primarily demographic and accounting data, but make little use of other financial data. In three companies visited, the industrial relations departments, which have primary responsibility for evaluating the financial impact of contract proposals, make extensive use of accounting, as well as demographic, data, but almost no use of other financial data. The industrial relations departments receive periodic reports which indicate both the total labor costs and their distribution among the various payroll accounts. In these companies, as well as in several of the companies which also make use of additional financial data, the reports serve as the basis for determining the cost of proposed contract changes.

The reports are prepared on a monthly, quarterly or semiannual basis and are usually submitted by each plant or division in the company. Typically, they indicate the number of hourly employees, the number of hours worked, the number of hours paid for and the distribution, by account, of the payroll costs. The reports prepared by each division of a chemical company, for example, require an indication of the cost of direct wages and of other forms of compensation. Other forms of compensation are divided into four classifications:

> *Group I benefits,* which are direct payments to employees based on time worked—for example, overtime premiums, shift differential premiums and call-in pay.
>
> *Group II benefits,* which are direct payments for time not worked—for example, holiday pay, military leave pay, and vacation pay.

Group III benefits, which are amounts charged to the division but not necessarily paid to the employees—for example, group insurance and pension charges.

Group IV benefits, which are statutory payments to the government—for example, FICA tax, state disability insurance tax, and unemployment insurance tax.

In those companies in which the industrial relations departments use primarily demographic and accounting data, the costs of contract changes are computed strictly on an historical basis. That is, the costs are figured on the implicit assumption that the levels of operations and relative mixes of straight-time hours, overtime hours, and second- and third-shift hours, as well as other variables, will remain constant. For example, in evaluating the cost of an additional holiday, such firms, unlike those which use only demographic data, would, as a starting point in their analyses, examine the amounts charged to holiday pay accounts in prior years and might take into account the amounts of production lost on previous holidays and how such lost production was recovered.

Firms that use all three types of data. The remaining firms make use of additional financial data in evaluating contract proposals—but to varying (and often inadequate) degrees. Managers responsible for evaluating contract proposals in these firms receive copies of corporate operational reports and projections and explicitly consider them in making contract decisions. Yet in all but one of these firms computations of contract costs are nevertheless based primarily on the use of labor in past periods. The managers indicated that unless the reports show substantial differences between projected use of labor and historical use of labor, they use the historical data.

The managers interviewed said that although they do not use the financial data in their calculations of contract costs, the data provide them with additional guidance. For example, one negotiator remarked that if the profit plan indicates that profits in the first year of the contract will be relatively low, he will attempt to delay a major portion of a wage increase until the later years. Another said that, in determining how much of an increase a particular division can afford, he pays particular attention to the expected ratio of labor costs to value of product manufactured. It is essential, he remarked, that he therefore be aware of anticipated production volume.

The approach toward contract analysis of one major manufacturer is considerably more far-reaching than that of any other firm studied. In this concern, all costs are computed using expected volume ("estimated planning volume") over the life of the contract.[4] The amount and detail of the data used by the company are substantially greater than those used by any of the other firms. The "estimated planning volume" serves as the foundation for all company plans and budgets. It indicates the anticipated production volume (by product and model), the number of labor hours needed and the expected level of employment. All estimates are broken down by months and by plant. Thus, in this company, the computation of the cost of an additional holiday takes into account the actual production planned for that particular day and the options available for making up the lost production.

Analysts in the finance department, which in this company is responsible for evaluating the financial impact of contract proposals, have access to payroll and personnel statistics via a computer terminal, and they are able to obtain required data, in usable form, within seconds. Seldom must they base computations on averages (e.g., average wage rate, average employee years of service) as is done in many other firms. Instead, they are able to use actual distributions whenever these are required for a more accurate computation. The department is further able to request that special surveys be taken to provide information that is not generated by the accounting records or maintained in the personnel files. For example, the accounting records indicate the amount of overtime paid in past years. But they do not reveal the breakdown of when such overtime was worked, e.g., Saturday, Sunday, or evenings. If the company is considering a change in overtime policy, such information is obviously needed. The company would survey one or more of its plants and generalize from the sample. No other company visited approached this one in the volume of data available to, and actually used by, contract analysts.

In another company, one which does a large part of its business with the government, the industrial relations department makes use of a great deal of other financial information but not to an-

---

[4] Term disguised to protect identity of firm.

TABLE 2.3

CORRELATION AMONG DEPARTMENTS REPRESENTED ON
BARGAINING TEAM, DEPARTMENTS WHICH DO MOST OF
FINANCIAL ANALYSES AND TYPES OF DATA USED

	Company				
	1	2	3	4	5
Is a representative of accounting or finance department on bargaining team?	No	Yes	Yes	Yes	Yes
Which departments do most of financial analyses?	Industrial Relations	Accounting and Industrial Relations	Accounting and Industrial Relations	Finance	Finance
What types of data are used?	Demographic and Accounting	Demographic, Accounting and Financial	Demographic, Accounting and Financial	Demographic, Accounting and Financial	Demographic, Accounting and Financial

	Company					
	6	7	8	9	10	11
Is a representative of accounting or finance department on bargaining team?	No	No	—[1]	No	No	No
Which departments do most of financial analyses?	Industrial Relations	Industrial Relations	Accounting	Corporate Compensation	Industrial Relations	Industrial Relations
What types of data are used?	Demographic and Accounting	Demographic	Demographic, Accounting and Financial	Demographic and Accounting	Demographic	Demographic

[1] Company engages in industry-wide bargaining. Bargaining team is composed of representative of three largest firms in industry.

alyze the financial impact of contract changes. Several months before negotiations begin, the industrial relations staff meets with accounting and finance representatives of the various corporate divisions. The industrial relations staff briefs the accounting and financial representatives on the anticipated cost of a contract settlement. The accounting and finance managers advise the industrial relations staff on the backlog of government contracts and forecasted operating results. The major purpose of the meeting from the standpoint of the finance and accounting representatives is to obtain input for profit plans; from the standpoint of the industrial relations staff it is to obtain information that will support the position it intends to take with the union—that the company is unable to afford its demands. The industrial relations department receives estimates of future volume. But it nevertheless computes the cost of contract changes using the historical, rather than anticipated, number of employees and hours worked.

As illustrated in Table 2.3, there is a correlation among the use of financial data and the departments which analyze the financial consequences of contract changes and the composition of the bargaining teams. In each of the firms that use financial data, and only in such firms, the accounting or finance department participates actively in preparation for bargaining. And significantly, in each of those firms (except for the one firm that engages in industry-wide bargaining) a representative of the accounting or finance department is a member of the negotiating team. Such firms are clearly more "finance oriented" than the others.

THE USE OF COMPUTERS IN PREPARATION
FOR COLLECTIVE BARGAINING

All of the firms visited use computers to maintain payroll and personnel records. Some also use computers to prepare special summaries of demographic and payroll data. But only two companies currently use computers to calculate the cost of specific contract changes. The remainder fail to make full use of the capabilities of their computers, and instead employ them as high-priced clerks.

In one of the two firms which use computers in cost analysis, the finance department has primary responsibility for analyzing contract proposals. The finance department places in computer storage payroll and demographic data, including wage rate distributions, age distributions and amounts charged to each payroll account. All data are broken down by plant. To compute the cost of a contract change, a financial analyst writes a computer program which calls upon the storage files for necessary source data.

Another firm has developed a program to compute the costs of several types of contract changes but it is currently being used by only one of several of its divisions. As do the programs used by the other company, it requires as input demographic and historical payroll data. The program has so far been developed to assist in answering only a limited number of questions. Among them are:

a. What would be the cost of granting a cents-per-hour increase as opposed to an across-the-board percentage increase?

b. What would be the cost of granting geographic pay differentials?

c. What would be the cost of granting an additional holiday?

The program presents answers in two forms: the direct cost of the change, and the "total employment" cost of the change. The direct cost is simply the total additional dollars required by the increase in the particular component of compensation. For example, the direct cost of a base-wage increase is the cents-per-hour increase times the total number of man-hours worked. The total employment cost is the direct cost plus the cost of increases in other benefits or taxes which are a function of the base-wage rate, such as holiday pay, overtime pay and FICA tax. The costs are expressed in cents per hour (i.e., total cost divided by man-hours worked). The algorithms used are straightforward and are founded on the assumption that historical levels of operations will be maintained in the future.

The manager who wrote the program admitted that the algorithms are sufficiently simple and the data base sufficiently small that a desk calculator could be substituted for the computer. But the primary value of the program, he quite properly noted, is that in writing and revising it, he is required to identify the interrelationships among the various components of compensation.

ACCOUNTS MAINTAINED SPECIFICALLY TO SUPPLY DATA TO BE USED IN COLLECTIVE BARGAINING

Although comprehensive contract evaluation requires information on a recurring basis that might not ordinarily be generated by traditional accounting systems, no official interviewed could cite any accounts maintained by his company specifically to provide data for collective bargaining. None could recall his firm even considering whether additional accounting data would facilitate contract evaluation.

Some accounts do, of course, provide data that is of primary interest to industrial relations officials. For example, all companies visited maintain accounts which indicate amounts paid for hours not worked (e.g., holiday pay, personal leave pay, jury duty pay). Such costs can generally be controlled only by the industrial relations department through changes in contract provisions.

But several industrial relations officials indicated that they often feel that the accounting systems of their firms fail to provide them adequate data with which to make bargaining decisions. One official recalled an instance when the union which represented his firm's employees demanded a change in corporate policy regarding overtime pay. Existing policy required that an employee working overtime be compensated for the overtime hours at time and one-half the rate applicable to the shift on which he worked the greater number of hours. The union requested that, in future, compensation for overtime be based on the rate applicable to the shift during which he worked the overtime hours, if such rate were higher than his normal rate. The accounting records of the firm provided insufficient information with which to estimate the cost of the change. The official was forced to obtain the necessary information on a sample basis. He suggested that in the future the industrial relations department might attempt to determine several months in advance what special data it would need to prepare for the forthcoming negotiations and request the accounting department to establish the necessary accounts for a period of several months prior to the start of bargaining.

Industrial relations officials seldom have an impact on the design of corporate accounting systems. As a consequence, such systems often fail to meet the information requirements of the collective bargaining process.

TWO SPECIAL CASES

Two special situations may be of interest to labor relations executives. The company visited which engages in coordinated bargaining with other firms in its industry has unusual problems of data collection and analysis. In this company's industry, a master agreement, which deals with major economic issues, is negotiated by a committee composed of two representatives of the largest company in the industry and one representative from each of the next two largest companies. Local agreements are negotiated independently by each company.

A change in the master agreement will obviously not have an identical financial impact on each of the firms in the coordinated bargaining unit. For example, the cost of a change in pension provisions will depend to a great extent on the age distribution of the employee population. A firm which has older plants will often have older employees. An immediate increase in pension benefits would, therefore, result in a greater cash outflow from the firm with older plants.

In the industry of the firm visited, contract changes are negotiated on the basis of how they will affect the single largest firm in the bargaining unit. This firm, as a result, has but limited influence on the outcome of bargaining. It is unable to seek the refinements in the contract that a company which bargains independently can. But the company does have two representatives—the same number as every other firm—on a bargaining coordinating committee. It participates in strategy meetings and must, in order to have its interests properly represented, be aware of the financial impact of proposed contract changes on itself. The company does, therefore, analyze all contract changes as though it were negotiating independently. Contract changes are analyzed jointly by the industrial relations and accounting departments, and the director of industrial relations receives reports of operating results and corporate plans. The major difference in the collection and analysis of data between this firm and independent firms is that the firm is required to file periodic reports of labor costs and provide various employee statistics to an industry institute.

The airline company also has unusual problems in evaluating the financial impact of labor contracts—especially those involving flight personnel. The formulas for computing wages of flight personnel are complex and the contracts contain a great many more work rules than are found in those of typical manufacturing firms. Changes in work rules may sometimes necessitate significant changes in personnel scheduling.

The compensation of pilots, for example, is composed primarily of flight pay. "Flight pay" means pay for actual hours flown, as well as, in some cases, pay for hours not flown but credited as if they were flown. It has several components:

longevity pay, which is based on the pilot's years of accredited service with the airline;

hourly pay, which is determined by the type of equipment flown and by whether the flying takes place during the day or the night;

gross weight pay, which is a function of the maximum certified weight of the aircraft flown;

mileage pay, which is computed according to a standard schedule of the normal miles per hour flown by various types of aircraft; and

accredited service pay, which is, in essence, a cents-per-hour bonus, the amount of which is based on aggregate service with the airline, for pilots who have at least 12 years' accredited service.

The contract establishes a maximum number of hours per month that pilots can fly and imposes restrictions on the scheduling of those hours. Pilots are allowed to select, on the basis of seniority, their "lines of flying" or flight schedules.

Evaluation of a flight contract could not possibly be conducted effectively solely by the labor relations department without substantial input from other departments in the company. Knowledge of the impact of changes in work rules on planned lines of flying, schedule changes and introduction of new aircraft is essential to a proper analysis.

In the airline visited, the labor relations department has overall responsibility for collective bargaining, but the finance department analyzes contract costs. Two analysts in the finance department are assigned to contract evaluation. One deals primarily with ground contracts (those involving, among others, machinists and communication workers); the other deals primarily with flight contracts (those involving pilots and stewardesses).

Major policy decisions are made, and bargaining strategy is formulated, by the labor relations department. The vice president of labor relations receives periodic reports on results of company operations and plans for the future. In making policy decisions he works closely with both the senior vice president of personnel, to whom he reports, and the president of the corporation.

The vice president of labor relations indicated that prior to the start of negotiations, the president, together with other members of top management, establishes guidelines for a settlement. In establishing such guidelines management looks primarily to settlements of other airlines and to anticipated economic conditions in the industry. As soon as the demands of the union are known, the labor relations department requests the finance department to determine their cost. The finance department has access to both accounting and personnel data, but it also works closely with the operations department. The operations department is in charge of personnel assignments and flight schedules. If, for example, the union requests a change in a work rule, the finance department will request an evaluation of its impact on operations. The operations department will attempt to "schedule around" the change by making minor adjustments in the lines of flying, but sometimes the change will require that additional pilots be hired or that currently employed pilots be trained on different types of aircraft. To the extent that personnel must be trained, the finance department must estimate the cost of such training. (It ignores the cost of hiring). Similarly, if the union demands an increase in the hourly pay for flying a specific type of aircraft, the finance department must get estimates of how many flight-miles are planned for that type of aircraft. Or, if the union proposes a change in company policy regarding amount of flight time credited or paid for hours not flown (e.g., "deadheading" or traveling as a passenger between airports), the finance department not only must obtain information on the number of hours involved, the years of service of the personnel affected, their rates of pay, and the like, but it must also be advised whether such a change would make certain lines of flying more attractive—and, as a result, more costly to the company—to senior pilots who have choice of lines of flying.

Because of the nature of flight contracts, airlines are virtually required to evaluate changes in labor contracts in terms of anticipated changes in the overall operations of the firm. They must do out of necessity what other firms should do by choice.

SUMMARY

The primary responsibility for collective bargaining is held by the industrial relations department. Cost information is supplied by an accounting or finance department upon request. Characteristically, the accounting or finance department plays a relatively passive role, furnishing data directly from payroll records, but occasionally the accounting or finance department is in charge of financial analysis. There is a close correlation between the degree of participation in the collective bargaining process of accounting and finance personnel and the comprehensiveness of the analysis performed. Those firms in which the function of the accounting or finance department is limited to supplying payroll data base their contract reviews largely on demographic or historical accounting data and ignore plans for the future. On the other hand, those firms in which the industrial relations department and the accounting or finance department cooperate closely (as exemplified by membership of a representative of the accounting or finance staff on the bargaining team) also introduce financial data into their analyses. Such information would include internal economic statistics of the type normally found in budgets or profit reports and often include projected, as well as historical, records of manpower requirements, revenues, production volume, product mix and non-labor costs.

A detailed review of the analytical procedures followed by the companies appears in the following two chapters.

CHAPTER III

Evaluating Wage Rates and Payments for Time Not Worked

In virtually all companies, direct wages constitute the single largest component of compensation. But as unions step up their efforts to win more leisure time and better working conditions for their members, payments for time not worked represent an increasing share of total labor costs. In costing contracts, the greater portion of managerial effort is likely to be devoted to examining changes in wages rates (including cost-of-living adjustments and premium pay) and compensation for nonproductive time such as vacations, holidays and relief time.

WAGE RATES

Direct Wages

Cents Per Hour

All negotiators interviewed agreed that their primary goal in bargaining is to minimize the cents-per-hour direct wage increase granted.[1]

---

[1] There are, of course, exceptions. The director of industrial relations of one company observed that the overall wage scale in his industry is lower than that in other industries within his firm's labor market. His firm must employ a small number of craftsmen whose skills are required in large numbers by other industries in the area. In order to hire such craftsmen, his firm must pay a competitive wage. In a recent bargaining session, his goal was to increase the wages of those few craftsmen and at the same time minimize the increases given to the rest of the firm's employees.

TABLE 3.1

SUMMARY OF PROCEDURES USED TO DETERMINE
CENTS-PER-HOUR COST OF DIRECT WAGE INCREASES

No. of Firms [1]	Procedure
2	Consider actual negotiated cents per hour to be the cents-per-hour cost. Add to such cost a "roll-up percentage" based upon prior years' experience.
7	Multiply negotiated cents-per-hour increase by average number of hours for which each man was paid in previous year and divide product by average number of productive hours (or an arbitrary number of hours such as 1,900 or 2,000) per man.
	Five firms add to cents-per-hour cost a "roll-up percentage" based upon recent years' experience.
	Two firms add to cents-per-hour cost both a "roll-up percentage" based upon recent years' experience and a "package roll-up percentage" which takes into account increases in benefits negotiated concurrently wtih increases in wages.

[1] Two firms negotiate in terms of percentage increases and do not compute cents-per-hour costs.

Surprisingly, however, a number of the many industrial relations officials interviewed appeared relatively indifferent toward the total cost, in dollars, of a direct wage increase. It is sometimes said that the one absolutely essential figure that every negotiator should have in his mind is what a wage increase of one cent per payroll hour will cost the company in thousands of dollars a year. Although all companies visited do, at some point prior to concluding negotiations, compute the overall dollar cost of a settlement, many negotiators do not consider such cost to be especially pertinent to their decisions. More revelant to them is the total cents-per-hour cost of the increase. They bargain in terms of cents per hour, and they are evaluated by their superiors in terms of cents per hour.

Only two of the 11 companies visited do not negotiate in terms of cents per hour. Instead they bargain with respect to percentage increases. One of the two is an airline, and its wage formula makes it impractical to negotiate in terms of cents per hour. The other is an oil company, which follows industry tradition in discussing percentage increases.

There are two basic methods by which firms determine the "direct" (i.e., ignoring the effect on other forms of compensation) cents-per-hour cost of a wage increase. The simpler procedure is to consider the negotiated cents-per-hour increase as the actual cost. Thus, the cost of granting a worker a 10-cents-per-hour increase is 10 cents per hour. Should increases of differing amounts be granted to employees in various job classifications, it is necessary to compute an average increase, weighted by the number of employees (or number of man-hours worked) in each job classification. For example, if a company offers 100 workers an increase of 10 cents per hour and 50 employees an increase of five cents per hour, the cents-per-hour cost would be 8.3 cents—a weighted average of the two increases.

The second and more widely used method takes cognizance of a firm's requirement to pay wages for a certain number of hours during which employees do not work. It expresses the cost of an increase in terms of cents per productive hour. The total increase in wages is divided by an estimated number of productive hours. For example, assume again that a firm grants a ten-cents-per-hour and a five-cents-per-hour wage increase. Assume also that in the previous year the firm paid for 22,000 hours of labor in the higher paid job classification and 11,000 hours in the lower paid job classification, but that it received only 20,000 and 10,000 productive hours respectively. The cents-per-hour cost of the direct wage increase would be $.0917, computed as follows:

$$
\begin{array}{ll}
22{,}000 \text{ hours x } \$0.10 = \$2{,}200 & \\
11{,}000 \text{ hours x } \$0.05 = \phantom{\$2{,}}550 & \$2{,}750 \\
\quad \text{Divided by productive} & \\
\quad \text{hours} & 30{,}000 \text{ hours} \\
\quad \text{Equals cents-per-hour cost} & \$0.0917 \\
\end{array}
$$

In determining the divisor, productive hours, most firms use the average number of productive hours during each year of the previous contract. Others use a standard figure, generally either 1,900 or 2,000 hours per employee.

"Roll-up"

The second method just described—the one by which total wage costs are divided by productive hours—indirectly takes into account the impact of the wage rate increase on a certain number of nonproductive time (such as relief time and down time) for which employees are compensated. But it ignores the impact of the increase on a number of fringe benefits, the costs of which are a direct function of the direct wage rate. Examples of some of these benefits are:

1. *Social Security and unemployment insurance contributions.* The employer's contribution is computed as a percentage of each employee's wage up to a fixed amount annually. To the extent that the annual earnings of some employees are less than the fixed amounts, an increase in wages will require an increase in Social Security and unemployment insurance contributions.

2. *Life insurance.* Often the amount of insurance coverage for which the employer pays is based on the annual earnings of the employee. As the earnings of the employee increase, so too will the amount and cost of the coverage.

3. *Overtime premium and shift premium.* Overtime premium is almost always, and shift premium is sometimes, computed as a percentage of base wages. As the base wage rate goes up, so also will required overtime and shift premiums.

4. *Pension benefits.* Pension benefits are often computed as a percentage of employees' average annual earnings over a number of years. An increase in wages will increase the cost of providing pension benefits.

All companies at which interviews were conducted recognize that an increase in direct wages will result in an increase in the cost of certain fringe benefits. The effect of the wage increase on fringe benefits is known by several terms: "roll-up," "creep," or "add-on."

One company uses a rule of thumb in determining the additional cost of wage increase attributable to "roll-up." It adds to the cost of the direct wage increase a fixed percentage of that cost. The same percentage has been used for several years, and it is not reviewed each contract. Other companies use a similar technique but, based on experience over the previous contract, recompute the roll-up percentage prior to each series of negotiations. The firms divide the amounts charged to specific benefit accounts (e.g., overtime premium, holidays, vacations and Social Security) by the amounts charged to the direct-wage accounts to obtain a new roll-up percentage.

In evaluating the financial impact of roll-up, only two companies interviewed recognize that roll-up percentages based on historical payroll data cannot properly be applied to the cost of anticipated direct-wage increases if fringe benefit increases are going to be negotiated at the same time as direct-wage increases. These two companies add to the cost of the direct-wage increase, not only an amount representing the increase in the cost of current fringe benefits resulting from the increase in the base-wage rate, but also an amount representing the increase in newly negotiated fringe benefits attributable to the change in the base-wage rate. The latter amount is computed by one of the two firms (the other follows an only slightly different procedure) by multiplying the cost of the direct-wage increase by a "package roll-up percentage." The package roll-up percentage represents the ratio of the cost of incremental changes in fringe benefits to that of direct-wage costs under the previous contract. The method used by the firm can be summarized as follows:

1. Using historical payroll data the firm determines the cost of both wages and those fringe benefits which are a function of the direct-wage rate.

2. It computes a roll-up percentage by dividing the cost of those fringe benefits which are a function of the direct-wage rate by the cost of the direct wages.

3. It determines the direct cost of the proposed increase in the base-wage rate.

4. It multiples the direct cost of the proposed increase in the base-wage rate by the roll-up percentage to obtain the increase in the cost of fringes attributable to the increase in the direct-wage rate.

5. It adds the resulting product to the direct cost of the proposed increase in the base-wage rate to determine the total of the direct cost of the increase in the base-wage rate and the cost of automatic increases in fringe benefits.

(Those firms using a historical roll-up percentage follow the same procedure up to this point. The remaining steps take into account changes in benefits currently being negotiated.)

6. The firm computes the cost of proposed increases in the benefits themselves which are currently being negotiated. It computes such costs using the *old* base-wage rate.

7. It determines the package roll-up percentage by dividing the cost of changes in benefits (per step 6) by the old direct-wage costs.

8. It computes the increase in costs of the new benefits, which will result because of the increase in the base-wage rate, by multiplying the package-roll percentage by the increased costs of the direct wages (per step 3).

9. It computes the total cost by adding the increase in costs of the new benefits (per step 8) to the total of the direct cost of the increase in the base-wage rate and the cost of automatic increases in fringe benefits (per step 5).

A simple example might be helpful. Assume that a firm currently pays its employees at the rate of $4.00 per hour and that the current cost of its fringe benefits is $1.00 per hour. The company is considering a wage increase of $0.80 per hour and increases in fringe benefits whose cost, based on the current wage rate, would be $0.40 per hour. Assume also that the company employs 500 men each of whom works 2,000 hours per year; the company uses 1,000,000 man-hours of labor per year. The cost of the increase in the base-wage rate would be computed as follows:

1. Cost of direct wages using old base-wage rate:
    $4.00 x 1,000,000 man-hours = $4,000,000

   Cost of fringe benefits using old base-wage rate:
    $1.00 x 1,000,000 man-hours = $1,000,000

2. Roll-up percentage:
    $1,000,000/$4,000.000 = 25%

3. Direct cost of the proposed increase:
    $0.80 x 1,000,000 man-hours = $800,000

4. Increase in cost of fringe benefits attributable to the increase in base-wage rate:
    $800,000 x 25% = $200,000

5. Cost of increase in direct wages and increase in fringe benefits attributable to increase in base-wage rate:
   $800,000 + $200,000 = $1,000,000

6. Cost of changes in contract provisions pertaining to fringe benefits, based on old wage rate:
   $0.40 x 1,000,000 man-hours = $400,000

7. Package roll-up percentage:
   $400,000/$4,000,000 = 10%

8. Increase in cost of proposed benefits attributable to increase in base-wage rate:
   $800,000 x 10% = $80,000

9. Total increase in costs:
   $1,000,000 (from step 5) + $80,000 = $1,080,000.

Thus, the total increase in cost attributable to the increase in the base-wage rate would be $1,080,000.

The additional steps (6 through 9) clearly improve the analysis. The ratio of the cost of fringe benefits to that of direct wages is not constant, and adjustments in fringe benefits will change the ratio. A roll-up percentage, for example, based on a contract which requires eight paid holidays would not be appropriate for determining the roll-up effect if the contract were changed to provide for 10 paid holidays. The package roll-up percentage takes into account the fringe-benefit increases being negotiated concurrently with wage increases.

A major problem in evaluating the cost of and negotiating direct wage increases is that of timing—how much of an increase should be granted in each year of a multi-year contract. The question of timing will be addressed in detail in Chapter V.

Cost-of-Living Adjustments

Cost-of-living adjustments, sometimes known as "escalator adjustments," are increases or decreases in wages based upon movements of a price index, usually the Consumer Price Index of the U. S. Bureau of Labor Statistics. Such adjustments are designed to protect the "real" wages of employees from the effects of inflation. A typical cost-of-living provision, for example, might require a one-cent-per-hour increase for each 0.4-point increase in the Con-

TABLE 3.2

SUMMARY OF ASSUMPTIONS USED TO EVALUATE
COST-OF-LIVING ADJUSTMENTS

No. of Firms [1]	Assumption
4	Firms assume that the maximum increase required by proposed contract provisions will be the actual increase they will have to grant.
4	Firms estimate the single "most likely" levels the price index will reach and assume wage increase will be either that required if index reaches such levels or the maximum, whichever is lower.

[1] Remaining three firms have never seriously negotiated cost-of-living adjustments and have, therefore, never evaluated them.

sumer Price Index. Sometimes an escalator clause will contain a "cap," or a provision establishing a maximum increase, either over the life of the contract or for each year of the contract. Often the clause will stipulate that a portion of any increase granted during a year will be added to the base-wage rate at the end of that year. Once the increase is added to the base-wage rate, wages are protected against a subsequent fall in the price index.

Cost-of-living adjustments present special analytical problems. The amount of increase to be granted over the life of the contract not only is variable but also is beyond the control of management. If there is not a cap on the adjustment, management cannot be certain of the wage rate at the end of the contract. If there is a cap, and it is set sufficiently low that it is likely to be reached, then management can be reasonably certain of the wage rate at the end of the contract, but it still cannot be sure of the timing of the increases during the contract.

Of eight companies interviewed which have recently evaluated the financial impact of a cost-of-living adjustment, four assume that the maximum increases they might be required to grant will be the actual increases that they will, in fact, grant. The remaining four estimate the most likely levels that the price index will reach and assume that the most likely increases will be the actual increases (provided, of course, that the increase does not exceed the cap). No firm even considers the possibility of a decline in the index. In only one of the firms which makes estimates of the levels that the price index will reach were such estimates made by an economics department; in the others they were made by members of the industrial relations staff.

Either one of the two assumptions could lead firms to make "incorrect" bargaining decisions. Firms that base their computations on the former assumption, that the maximum increase will be the actual increase, are able to avoid the task of projecting the trend of consumer prices—a frustrating task for even the most erudite economists. Indeed, executives of all four companies which make this assumption do so on the ground that the projections that would otherwise have to be made are subject to unacceptable degrees of error. They take it for granted that the increase in the consumer price index to the level associated with the maximum increase (either annually or over the life of the contract) will be immediate. They ignore the question of when, or by how much, wages will actually have to be increased. Therefore, they overstate the expected cost of the escalator clause and, perhaps as a result, forego opportunities to trade smaller increases in the base-wage rate or in fringe benefits for additional—and less costly—increases in the cost-of-living adjustment.

The firms that base their computations on the latter assumption, that the consumer price index will follow a "most likely" pattern, may avoid the error of overstating the possible cost. But they are nevertheless likely to ignore the possible cost of extreme, although less probable, changes in the price index. The best estimate of the firm, for example, might be price-level increases of 5 percent annually. Increases of 2 percent and 10 percent might be considered unlikely, but nevertheless possible. The wage increase required by the 10-percent price rise (assuming no cap) might be disastrous to the firm, especially if competitors were not required to make comparable wage adjustments. Such possibilities should surely be taken into account in evaluating the financial impact of cost-of-living adjustments. Several appropriate techniques for doing so are described in the literature of decision-making under conditions of uncertainty.[2]

---

[2] See, for example, Howard J. Riaffa, DECISION ANALYSIS, INTRODUCTORY LECTURES ON CHOICES UNDER UNCERTAINTY (Reading, Massachusetts: Addison-Wesley, 1968), and Robert Schlaifer, ANALYSIS OF DECISIONS UNDER UNCERTAINTY (New York: McGraw-Hill, 1969).

Overtime Premiums and Shift Differentials

TABLE 3.3

SUMMARY OF ASSUMPTIONS USED TO EVALUATE THE COST
OF OVERTIME PREMIUMS AND SHIFT DIFFERENTIALS

No. of Firms	Assumption
10	Number of hours paid at premium rates will be the same as in prior years.
1	Number of hours paid at premium rates will be that required by anticipated production volume.

It is a widely accepted practice in the United States to pay workers both a premium for working hours in addition to the normal number of hours per day or week, and a "shift differential," usually stated in cents per hour, for working either an evening or a night shift.

Several issues relating to overtime pay and shift differentials are continually faced by the firms interviewed. Union demands that employees be paid doubletime or even tripletime for working during what they consider particularly unpleasant periods (e.g., Saturdays, Sundays and holidays) or periods after they have already worked 12 consecutive hours are frequent subjects for negotiations. Since shift differentials are not usually a fixed percentage of the wage rate, the amounts of the differentials are also bargaining issues.

All but one of the firms studied compute the cost of a change in contract provisions relating to overtime premium or shift differential on the assumption, often tenuous, that the number of hours of overtime or non-day-shift labor will be approximately the same during each year of the new contract as during the last year of the old. The one firm that is the exception follows a more comprehensive procedure and attempts to estimate the number of hours for which it will have to pay premium rates during the term of the contract. The estimates are based upon the firm's "estimated planning volume," a forecast, by month, of production volume. A financial analyst, using estimated volume, is able to determine, within wide ranges, the approximate number of overtime and second- and third-shift labor hours that will be required. The firm does not, however, modify the forecasted production schedules to reflect anticipated cost changes attributable to the new contract provisions themselves. The financial analyst recognized that such an extension of the analysis might be theoretically desirable, but he pointed out that the firm's planning model is insufficiently sensitive to be affected by minor contract changes. Too many other variables affect production planning for changes in overtime or shift-differential provisions—unless they force a major change in policy—to have an impact on scheduling.

Whether a firm can properly assume that its mix of labor hours compensated for at straight-time and premium rates (herein referred to as the labor-rate mix) will remain constant is a function of both the stability of the demand for its products and the extent to which increases in production volume require increases in labor. If the demand for the firm's product is stable, or if labor requirements are fixed relative to production volume, it is likely that the labor-rate mix of the firm will also remain constant. Some firms, often in capital-intensive industries such as oil, chemical and glass, maintain 24-hour continuous-process operations, and the number of employees required to operate the plants remains relatively unchanged regardless of volume. Overtime is generally required of production workers only to replace workers who are absent or on vacation and of maintenance workers only to make emergency repairs. For several of the firms studied, the assumption of a constant labor-rate mix is clearly invalid. Historically, the number of overtime hours has varied from year to year. For others, the assumption is valid, but is obviously being made without examination of the underlying rationale.

Once the firm determines the number of labor hours which would be affected by a change in contract provisions pertaining to overtime or shift differentials, computation of the cost of such changes presents no special problems. The cost is simply the number of hours times the change in rates, plus, of course, any changes in taxes or benefits which might be a function of gross pay.

Unfortunately, even firms in which the labor-rate mix remains stable may have difficulty ascertaining the number of hours affected by a contract change. Traditional accounting records may indicate only the total amounts paid in overtime or shift differentials and not the reason (e.g., hours were worked on Saturday, holidays, evenings) why the overtime premium and shift differentials were paid. Managers interviewed cited several questions to which they are unable to obtain answers from accounting records: How many hours of compensation would be affected if the firm was required to (1) pay doubletime after 12 hours of work; (2) pay doubletime or tripletime for work on Saturdays, Sundays and holidays; and (3) pay day-shift workers at time and one-half the evening-shift rate, rather than the day-shift rate, for overtime work performed during the evening shift? Industrial relations officers indicated that when faced with such questions they either make an "intuitive" assessment of the number of hours involved or survey their plants. Sometimes the survey is nothing more than a call to several plant managers; at other times it is based upon statistically valid sampling techniques.

Surprisingly, most accounting systems could be adapted to provide the required information at minimum additional cost. Seldom, unfortunately, do industrial relations executives even think to discuss their data needs with the company accountants.

In firms in which the labor-rate mix does not remain stable, the task of determining the number of hours affected by a contract change may be substantially more difficult. Managers of such firms often pay considerable attention, throughout the lives of their contracts, to the problem of determining optimum levels of employment. They are continually faced with decisions as to whether to hire additional workers or to request that current employees work overtime; whether to recall laid-off workers or work on an overtime basis; and whether to add additional shifts or extend existing shifts. In making their determinations, the managers must consider the terms of their labor contracts—specifically those provisions pertaining to overtime rates, shift differentials and benefits to laid-off employees. The financial impact of changes in those same contract provisions, however, is dependent upon determinations to be made throughout the life of the contract—those of the number of hours that must be compensated for at premium rates. In estimating the financial impact of contract changes, the firm must, therefore, take into account not only its anticipated production volume, but also its plans for fulfilling that volume. Often, as in the case of the one company which does base cost computations on anticipated, rather than historical, patterns of labor use, the contract changes will not be sufficiently significant to have an impact on scheduling. But the possibility that it might should at least be considered.

The experience of one company demonstrates the importance of considering the amount of overtime to be worked during the life of a contract. The company acceded to a union demand that vacation pay be computed as a percentage of gross pay, rather than as a percentage of net base pay. The company's use of overtime increased substantially both during the life of the contract and in subsequent years, and as a result the cost of paid vacations increased far more than the company had anticipated. The director of industrial relations cited this contract change as a major error that he had made—one that he possibly could have avoided had he explicitly considered the use of overtime that the firm's planned production volume would require.

PAYMENTS FOR TIME NOT WORKED

Vacations

TABLE 3.4

SUMMARY OF PROCEDURES USED TO DETERMINE ANNUAL
COST OF INCREASES IN NUMBER OF DAYS OF VACATION

No. of Firms	Procedure
4	Multiply number of additional vacation hours by base-wage rates.
3	Multiply number of additional vacation hours by amounts charged to vacation accounts in past year divided by number of productive hours in past year.
3	Make general assumption as to how lost time will be made up. Multiply number of additional vacation hours by cost per hour of making up lost time.
1	Estimates amount of lost production and specifically determines number of workers who will have to be replaced, who will have to work overtime at time and one-half base-wage rate, and who will have to work overtime at twice base-wage rate. Multiplies number of additional hours for which employees will have to be compensated by appropriate rates.

Corporations grant vacations, in the words of one labor agreement, "to promote good will by providing vacations with pay for

wage earner employees in recognition of their regular and continuous service over a number of years, and to enable those employees
who qualify to enjoy a period of rest." Contract terms pertaining
to vacations must deal with three issues:

1. *Eligibility.* Who is eligible to receive a vacation and to how
   many days is an employee entitled?

2. *Scheduling.* When can an employee take his vacation?

3. *Payment.* How much will an employee be paid while he is
   on vacation?

Most contracts require an employee be employed for a minimum period of time—often six months or a year—before he is
eligible for a vacation. The amount of vacation to which he is
entitled is usually determined according to a sliding scale of years
of service with the company; the longer the service with the company, the longer the vacation.

Contracts generally establish policies for the scheduling of
vacations which enable employees to have the greatest possible
choice in selecting a vacation period consistent with the production
requirements of management. Policies pertaining to vacation schedules have important financial implications since they can influence
the amount of production, the size of the workforce, and the amount
of overtime required. But in many companies, issues involving
vacation scheduling have been settled by prior labor agreements
and, as a result, are seldom given explicit financial consideration.
The master agreements usually contain statements of policy regarding scheduling, but actual rules are established at the plant level.
The most prevalent policy regarding vacation pay is to give workers time off without the loss of income that they would otherwise
earn. But since employees do not earn the same amounts each
week that they work, the amounts to which they are entitled are
not always readily apparent. Some firms pay employees for eight
hours per vacation day at their base-wage rates. But such policy
ignores any overtime pay employees might lose while they are on
vacation. Other firms compute vacation pay as a percentage of
employees' gross pay (that is, total wages earned including overtime premium), or as a number of hours of vacation times employees' average rates of pay, for the year preceding the period during
which employees are eligible to take their vacations. The average

rates of pay are determined by dividing the total pay received by each employee (including overtime pay and pay for time not worked) by the total number of hours paid for.

Contract changes most frequently proposed by unions involve increases in the amount of vacation pay and in the number of days of vacation. Normally the first step in evaluating changes in vacation policy is to determine the number of employees in each category of years of service (e.g., less than two years, two to five years, etc.), the number of additional days to which they will be entitled and (in most cases) the rates at which they will be paid. Thereafter, as was indicated in Table 3.4, some firms simply multiply the number of additional vacation hours by appropriate base wage rates while others compute the average cents-per-hour cost of a vacation hour per the historical accounting records and multiply that by the number of additional vacation hours. A few firms, however, pay primary attention, not to the amount of vacation pay that the employee will draw, but rather to the cost of maintaining production at planned volumes in spite of the additional vacation days. Most of these firms make general assumptions as to how any lost production might be made up. For example, one firm assumes all vacation hours will result in lost production and that such lost production should have to be made up by employees working overtime at premium rates. Another also assumes that all vacation hours would result in lost production but estimates that only some would have to be made up by employees working overtime. The remainder would be made up by temporary summer employees working at straight-time rates. Only one firm interviewed makes detailed analyses of the number of employees whose absence would be unlikely to decrease production, the number that would have to be replaced by workers compensated at overtime rates (both at time and one-half and at doubletime) and the number that could be replaced by temporary employees.

In the remainder of this section the procedures followed will be evaluated in the light of several situations actually faced by the firms studied:

1. *Additional vacation time will have no impact on production volume; the workers on vacation will not be replaced.* All companies interviewed have some workers who will not be replaced. Maintenance workers, for example, often are in this category. There

may be sufficient slack within a maintenance crew that, for short periods of time, the condition of equipment will not suffer if the crew is short-handed. The cost to the company of granting additional days of vacation will, therefore, be near zero.

2. *In order to fulfill production requirements, the company will require either nonvacationing employees to work overtime or vacationing employees to make up "lost" time by working overtime prior to or after their vacations.* In either case, the cost to the company will not be the vacation pay; it will be the overtime pay. Two companies, in addition to the one cited above, explicitly recognize this fact. One company computes the cost of additional vacation hours as 1.75 times each employee's base-wage rate. The company assumes that approximately one half the lost hours will be made up by employees working overtime at time and one-half their base rates and one half by employees working overtime at twice their base rates. The other firm assumes that all lost time will be made up at time and one-half.

3. *In order to fulfill production requirements the company will hire additional personnel on either a temporary or a permanent basis.* Several companies hire temporary employees, generally college students, as substitutes for vacationing permanent employees. The firms are required, by union contract, to pay the temporary employees according to the union wage scale. Several industrial relations managers observed that the primary advantage of hiring college students is that they are either ineligible for many fringe benefits because of the requirement of a minimum period of service, or they do not remain on the job sufficiently long to take advantage of available benefits. All of the firms which hire temporary help compute the cost of additional vacation days by multiplying the number of hours for which they will pay the temporary employees by the wage rate they will receive. But no company explicitly recognizes the costs of hiring the replacement workers. Yet the cost of putting new men on—and removing them from—the payroll can be great. Among the costs that are often overlooked are the following:

advertising
employment agencies
letters of application
application blanks
interviews by personnel department

interviews by line managers
security and credit investigations
references
company badges and safety equipment
indoctrination and training
break-in time
exit interviews
severance pay
extra Social Security taxes
increases in unemployment insurance costs [3]

One company, which computes the cost of additional vacation days on the basis of the wages of the employees taking vacations, has a special job classification for workers assigned to replace vacationing and absent men. The industrial relations director indicated that it would be unlikely that a small increase in the number of vacation days would necessitate an increase in the size of the firm's replacement crew. Hence, the cost of granting such an increase would be negligible. The company nevertheless considers the cost to be the wages that will be paid to the vacationing employees—and it thereby overstates the cost of the contract change.

One major company visited recently adopted an "extended vacation plan," under which senior employees are given periodic vacations of up to 13 weeks. Such a plan should cause no special problem of cost evaluation. However, when a worker is away from his job for such a lengthy period, it is likely that he will have to be replaced by an additional employee; it would be improbable in an efficiently managed organization that other members of his department could "pick up the slack" for such an extended period of time. Hence, the cost to the company will almost certainly be that of hiring and maintaining additional employees.

4. *A number of employees eligible for additional vacation days will exercise their option to work on, and receive pay for, the extra days.* In many companies, some employees choose to earn additional pay rather than take time off. In some companies, in fact, only a small number of employees actually use all their vacation days. In others, especially those which discontinue operations for a two-week period during the summer, most employees take the

---

[3] Frederick J. Gaudet, LABOR TURNOVER: CALCULATION AND COST, AMA Research Study 39 (New York: American Management Association, 1960), p. 39.

time off. To the extent that employees will accept payment for the additional vacation days, the cost to the company is relatively easy to compute. It will be the total number of dollars paid to the employees, plus any resultant increases in taxes and benefits, less the amounts that would normally be paid.

A fifth situation, although not faced by any of the firms studied, is also possible:

The company is operating at maximum capacity and, because of special skill requirements, will be unable to hire additional workers. An increase in the number of vacation days will result in a decline in production. The cost to the company will be, therefore, the variable profit on the goods that it would have been able to produce had it not granted the additional days of vacation.

Holidays

TABLE 3.5

SUMMARY OF PROCEDURES USED TO DETERMINE ANNUAL
COST OF ADDITIONAL HOLIDAYS

No. of Firms	Procedure
3	Multiply number of hours of additional holiday by appropriate base-wage rates.
4	Take appropriate percentage of amount charged to holiday pay account in previous year.
2	Estimate number of employees who will not work on holiday and number who will. Multiply number of hours of additional holiday granted to employees who will not work on holiday by appropriate base-wage rates and number of hours of additional holiday granted to those who will work by time and one-half (or twice) appropriate base-wage rates.
2	Estimate amount of lost production and specifically determine number of man-hours at straight time and premium rates that will be required to make up lost production. Multiply number of hours by appropriate rates. Add to total additional wages, cost of capital required to expand physical facilities.

The problem of evaluating the financial impact of an additional holiday is similar to that of evaluating that of an extra day of vacation. Both vacation and holiday benefits involve pay for time not worked.

Firms in some industries, such as chemicals and oil, are unable to discontinue operations on holidays. As a result, they require many of their employees to work on holidays and they must pay them at special rates, usually time and one-half or double their normal rates. They may allow maintenance and service personnel to take off on holidays, but they usually maintain production at, or near, normal volume.

Firms in industries which do not have continuous operations have greater flexibility in determining their level of production on holidays. They can shut down completely, operate at a fraction of normal volume, or operate at 100 percent of normal volume. If they operate at less than 100 percent of normal volume, however, they lose production and presumably have to make up such production at some other date. If the firm is operating at less than capacity, it has the same options available to make up lost production attributable to a holiday as it does to make up that lost because of vacations, with one important exception. It is seldom feasible for a firm to hire temporary employees for only one, or even several, days.

Most firms fail to consider either the number of employees who can be expected to work on holidays or how they will make up lost production. To compute the cost of an additional holiday, some firms simply multiply the number of additional holiday hours by the employee wage rates, while others divide the total amount in the holiday pay account of the previous year by the number of holidays granted in that year. The amount in the holiday pay account, however, may be a conglomerate of amounts paid to both employees who worked on the holidays and those who did not. Therefore, it provides little guidance for determining the incremental payments attributable to the holidays.

Two of the firms make assumptions as to the number of employees who will work, rather than take off the holidays. These firms recognize that the employees who work on the holiday will have to be compensated at premium rates, either time and one-half or double their normal rates. One firm simply assumes that all hourly employees will work on the holiday; the other assumes that the same percentage of employees who reported to work on similar holidays in the past will report to work in the future. They compute the cost of the additional holiday by multiplying the number of hours of holiday by the appropriate rates, either straight time, time and one-half, or doubletime.

Only two firms expand their analyses to give explicit consideration to how they will recover lost production. One of these firms follows an unusual procedure in computing the cost of a holiday. The firm usually ceases operations on holidays. It is unable to require employees to work overtime and generally has difficulty in persuading them to do so voluntarily. Production volume is a direct function of labor hours, and lost production cannot be recouped by increasing production during normal working hours on other days. For practical purposes, therefore, the firm is operating at capacity and can make up lost production only by expanding its plant and hiring additional workers. To compute the cost of a holiday, the firm adds to anticipated payroll costs estimated interest charges on the capital required to finance construction of the additional plant facilities necessary to maintain current levels of production. The firm's analysis of a proposal to add one holiday in 1973 might appear as:

Total amount charged to holiday pay account in 1972:	$3,000,000
Total man-hours worked in 1972:	22,000,000 hrs.
Cents-per-hour cost of 10 holidays in 1972 ($3,000,000 ÷ 22,000,000 hours):	$0.1364
Cents-per-hour cost of 10 holidays based on 15 percent wage increase to be granted in 1973 ($0.1364 x 1.15):	$0.1569
Cents-per-hour cost of one holiday based on 15 percent wage increase to be granted in 1973 ($0.1569 ÷ 10 holidays):	$0.0157
Additional holiday cost resulting from $200,000 in interest charges that would be incurred in order to finance additional plant required to offset lost production ($200,000 ÷ 22,000,000 hours):	$0.0091

Cents-per-hour cost of additional holiday, including interest charges
   ($.0157 + $0.0091): $0.0248

The cents-per-hour cost of an additional holiday would, therefore, be $0.0248, assuming that the firm will continue to operate at a volume requiring 22,000,000 labor hours. The interest charges that would be incurred ($200,000 in the example) were arrived at by multiplying the anticipated cost of required production facilities by the firm's "cost of capital." The anticipated cost of required production facilities was determined by multiplying the number of units produced per day by the firm's "cost of capacity"—the cost of plant facilities required to produce one unit of output. Both the cost of capital and the cost of capacity are determined by the firm's finance department.

The other firm that explicitly considers how it will make up lost production is the one which bases all labor projections on its estimated planning volume. The estimated planning volume indicates budgeted volume for each month, so the financial analyst who evaluates the cost of the holiday is able to estimate the number of units that would otherwise be produced on the proposed holiday. By comparing scheduled volume for the month with volume at practical capacity, the analyst can determine whether it would be feasible to make up the lost production during normal working hours on other days, or whether overtime will be required. He computes the cost of the holiday by multiplying the required number of overtime hours by time and one-half (or twice) the appropriate wage rates. Since the firm is not operating at maximum capacity, he does not have to consider the costs that would be incurred if additional facilities would have to be constructed.

Two officials interviewed cited experiences of their own firms which demonstrate the necessity of taking into account the timing of additional holidays. One industrial relations manager indicated his company has discovered that holidays that are "back to back" are considerably less costly than those that are spaced apart. In his industry furnaces must be shut down when plants discontinue operations for a holiday and rekindled when they reopen. Shutdown and start-up costs are relatively high. It is the strategy of his firm, he observed, to schedule all new holidays between Christmas and New Year's Day, and he anticipates that within a few years his firm will close for that entire week.

A financial analyst recalled that a union proposal to grant additional year-end holidays had corporate income tax implications that were not readily apparent. Under the proposal, employees would have holidays from December 24th through January 1st. But company policy requires that an employee must report for work on his last scheduled workday before the holiday and his first after the holiday in order to be eligible for holiday pay. Internal Revenue regulations, however, prescribe that in order for a firm to deduct accrued holiday pay as an expense, its employees must have satisfied all conditions of eligibility for holiday pay. Under the proposal, employees would not have met the eligibility requirements for pay for any of the holidays until at least January 2nd, the first working day after the holiday. Thus, the company would be unable to deduct any of the holiday pay until the end of the year in which the employees return to work. Previously, several workdays were scheduled between Christmas and New Year's Day so that at least a portion of the holiday pay was deductible in the earlier year. Since a tax deduction delayed is, in effect, a tax increase, there would be an additional cost to scheduling the new holidays at year end as opposed to any other time of the year.

Relief Time

TABLE 3.6

SUMMARY OF PROCEDURES USED TO DETERMINE ANNUAL
COST OF INCREASES IN RELIEF TIME

No. of Firms [1]	Procedure
2	Make "subjective" evaluation. Do not compute cost.
4	Multiply total hours of additional relief time by appropriate base wage rates.
1	Uses special relief time formula.

[1] Four firms did not recently negotiate changes in amount of relief time.

Rest periods, or relief time, seldom represent a major labor cost. Nevertheless, the problem of determining the financial impact of increases in rest periods illustrates some of the inherent difficulties of assessing contract provisions involving pay for time not worked.

Of the firms which have recently negotiated changes in contract provisions pertaining to relief time, all but one either consider the cost implications too immaterial to determine or simply multiply the total number of additional man-hours of relief time by the appropriate base-wage rates. One firm uses a special formula to compute the number of additional men that it will be required to hire if it increases the number or duration of rest periods and multiplies the number of such additional men by their anticipated total compensation.

The firm that uses the formula operates assembly lines and maintains special crews of relief men to substitute for employees on their breaks. The formula used is:

$$M = \frac{(\quad N \quad)e}{\dfrac{P}{R+S} - 1}$$

where:

M = number of additional employees that would have to be hired;

N = number of employees currently on the work force;

P = length of the period, in minutes, during which breaks can be taken;

R = proposed number of additional minutes of relief time;

S = "slippage," or the number of minutes needed for a relief man to move between assignments;

e = percent off standard, or 1 plus (or minus) the percent error in the past.

Assume, for example, that the union demands that ten minutes be added to the morning coffee break. There are currently 1,000 men employed in the plant and breaks are taken in the 180 minutes between 8 a.m. and 11 a.m. Since the ten minutes are to be added to the employees' existing break periods, additional "slippage," or time the relief men need to move between stations, would be zero. In the past, the firm has found that approximately 5 percent more relief men than indicated by the formula (without consideration of the "error factor") have been required.

According to the equation, the firm would have to hire an additional 62 employees, computed as follows:

$$\frac{(\ \ \frac{1,000}{180}\ \ )\ 1.05}{\frac{180}{180+0}-1} = 61.8$$

To view the formula from a slightly different perspective: Each employee would be away from his station 10/180 or 5.6 percent of the time during the period between 8 a.m. and 11 a.m. Therefore, an additional 5.6 percent of 1,000 employees, or 56 new relief men, would have to be hired. But, in addition, each relief man, himself, requires a break during the same period. So another 5.6 percent of the 56 new relief men, or three more men, must be hired. According to the basic formula, therefore, 59 men must be hired. Since the firm's experience indicates that the basic formula has understated its requirements by 5 percent, an additional 5 percent of 59 men, or another three men, must be hired. Hence the total of 62 men.

The cost of acceding to the union demand would, therefore, be that of hiring and compensating the 62 new employees. This cost would be reduced by the value of any work that the relief men might perform during the hours in which breaks are not scheduled. In the firm which uses the formula, the relief men work at odd jobs during the hours when breaks are not scheduled, but the firm has found that their productive contribution is too small to measure.

The firms that multiply total number of additional man-hours by appropriate base-wage rates implicitly assume that the additional relief time will cause a decline in production and that such decline will be offset by additional man-hours of labor compensated at straight-time rates. Their assumptions may be correct; whether they are or not depends primarily upon the production process they employ. But there are reasons to suggest that they are not:

1. The productivity of many employees, including almost all workers who are not on an assembly line, is not a direct function of time on the job. Employees have considerable leeway in adjust-

ing their required output to the time available. Maintenance workers, for example, are often "on call" to repair any breakdowns. An additional ten minutes of relief time is unlikely to affect the total amount of work they perform. Some production workers may be responsible for conducting routine tests and monitoring series of gauges. While they are on a break other employees can "cover" for them without loss of production.

2. Additional rest time may actually increase production if the efficiency of the employees is improved while they are actually at work. The physical and psychological effects of rest time are uncertain and difficult to measure, but it is probable that rest time has some impact on both morale and endurance, and hence on efficiency. Also, as one industrial relations manager pointed out, it is possible that if a union demand for additional rest time is not granted, the employees will take it anyway in "extra-legal" fashion.

3. To the extent that production is lost, it is unlikely that it can be recovered by a number of additional hours, which would be paid at straight time, exactly equal to the number of hours lost. If operations on an entire production line cease while workers are on their break, then the lost time can be made up either by placing in service additional equipment and hiring new employees, or by requiring current employees to work additional hours. Few firms are likely to place in service additional equipment or hire new employees because of an increase in relief time. Decisions to do so are generally made on the basis of more significant factors. And if employees work additional hours, it is probable that they will have to be paid at premium rates. If, instead of shutting down assembly lines during break periods, the firm replaces a few workers at a time with special relief men, the total number of hours for which the relief men are paid will seldom equal the number of hours of total relief time granted.

Miscellaneous Time Off

The contracts of almost all firms provide that employees shall be compensated for miscellaneous absences, such as those attributable to jury service, death in a family and short-term military duty. Generally such payments constitute a very small percentage of overall labor costs and changes in the amounts of payment or the requirements for eligibility are either infrequently negotiated or seldom an issue over which there is a dispute. Companies normally maintain special accounts in which the amounts paid for each type of absence are recorded, and such accounts are usually the primary source of information on the degree to which employees avail themselves of the benefits.

When considering a change in the amount of payment for a particular type of absence, firms commonly assume that the historical pattern of absences will be unaffected by the contractual change—i.e., that employees will not take additional days off because the compensation for such days has been increased. When considering a change in eligibility rules, they have to rely upon their own, usually highly subjective, estimates of the number of employees and labor hours affected by the change. Most firms studied do not believe that the dollar amounts involved justify comprehensive statistical analyses. One firm, in fact, automatically adds two cents to the cents-per-hour cost of every contract to take care of increases in miscellaneous benefits.

Where absolute, if not relative, dollar amounts are great, a casual attitude toward minor contract changes cannot be justified, however. The total labor costs of one firm, for example, are considerably greater than those of the other firms, and the dollar costs of even minor contract changes are likely to be substantial. A financial analyst in the firm gave an example of the detailed procedure he followed in computing the cost of a seemingly insignificant contract change—one which would extend bereavement benefits (of up to three days' pay) to cover deaths of employees' grandparents.

First, the analyst consulted actuarial tables to determine, from the actual age distribution of the employee population, the probable number and age distributions of employees' living grandparents. Then, again using actuarial tables, he determined the number of grandparents who could be expected to die during the next contract period. Next, he estimated from past experience the number of days bereaved employees were likely to take off (not all employees who are eligible for bereavement pay take the maximum number of days to which they are entitled). Finally, he determined the total number of hours for which the bereaved employees would have to be paid and, using an appropriate distribution of wage rates, computed the pay that they would receive.

Many labor contracts provide that once an employee reports to work he is entitled to be paid for a minimum number of hours. Sometimes a firm might call in an employee to make emergency repairs; at other times a piece of equipment might break down, thereby eliminating the need for its operator's services. In many instances, the firm either has no other productive work for the employee or is prevented by its labor agreement from assigning him to other tasks. Thus, it must pay the employee for time not worked. Such payments are generally referred to as "call-in payments."

The most common bargaining issue relating to call-in pay is the number of hours for which employees should be paid for reporting to work. In each firm at which changes in call-in pay were recently negotiated officials interviewed indicated that they assume that the number of occasions for which they must pay employees for calling in will be approximately the same in future years as it was in past years. To the extent that they have data available on the number of instances when call-in payments had to be made, they compute the additional cost as the product of the number of occasions, the number of additional hours, and the appropriate wage rates.

Some firms visited are required to pay selected employees for time spent on union business. Those that had occasion to evaluate the cost of a contract change involving payments for time spent on union business computed the cost by multiplying the number of additional hours for which payment would be required by the appropriate wage rates. None of the officials considered contract clauses dealing with either call-in pay or pay for union business worthy of additional analysis.

CHAPTER IV

Evaluating Other Contract Provisions

As the number of benefits included in labor agreements increases, the task of the labor relations manager becomes more complex. In addition to examining provisions dealing with wages and compensated time off, the contract analyst must also concern himself with those pertaining to pensions, accident and sickness insurance, supplementary unemployment benefits, job classifications and inequity funds. He must take into account not only the cost of increasing the compensation of workers who are covered by the contract, but also the effects of "spillover" or increases that will likely be granted to exempt employees. Moreover, the contract analyst must consider the interrelationship between labor costs and such "economic variables" as production volume, prices, product mix and capital investment.

INDIRECT BENEFITS

Pensions

Although pension plans were introduced into the U. S. industrial environment before the turn of the twentieth century, only in the last 25 to 30 years have both labor and management accepted the obligation of an employer to compensate his employees beyond the dates of their retirement. In the early stages of the development of the pension movement, pensions were widely recognized as gratuitous and discretionary payments by employers to faithful and long-serving employees. Today, however, provisions for pensions

are incorporated into over 90 percent of labor contracts in manufacturing industries.

The key problem of determining the cost of a pension plan is
that the total amount paid to each employee cannot be known with
certainty until he is dead. The eventual cost of a pension plan is a
function of many variables—none easily predictable—including
employee longevity, employee turnover, earnings on investments in
the pension fund and employee decisions as to when to retire.

Most companies avoid to some extent the problems of determining the cost of proposed changes in pension plans by assigning the task to consulting actuaries, although larger firms sometimes
employ "in-house" actuaries as well. The firms provide the actuaries with necessary demographic data, and the actuaries return
to them estimates of annual costs, expressed either in total dollars
or cents per labor hour.

In every firm visited, the annual cost considered relevant in
evaluating contract changes is that of the required cash contribution
the pension fund. All but one company "funds" its entire pension
accrual, so that the amounts charged to income on the financial
statements are identical to those of the cash payments. The firm
that is the exception does not necessarily contribute to its fund the
entire amount accrued, and it records as a current liability in its
position statement the excess of the amount accrued over the contribution to the fund.

The pension expense determined by an actuary depends not
only on his assumptions regarding longevity, retirement ages, earnings of investments and employee turnover, but also on his choice
of "actuarial cost method" ("a particular technique for establishing the amount and incidence of the annual actuarial cost accrual
for pension plan benefits, or benefit and expenses, and the related
actuarial liability." [1]). A few of the more widely used methods
which are acceptable under Accounting Principles Board Opinion
No. 8 are: (1) the entry-age normal method; (2) the individual
level-premium method; (3) the aggregate method; and (4) the
attained-age normal method. Selection of any one of the four
methods would yield a different pension accrual (and cash con-

---

[1] Ernest L. Hicks, ACCOUNTING FOR THE COST OF PENSION PLANS, Accounting Research Study No. 8 (New York: American Institute of Certified Public
Accountants, 1965), p. 139.

tribution to the pension fund) than would selection of another. If the actuary uses the entry-age normal method, the most widely used of the four, he must also decide on the number of years over which to amortize "prior service cost" (cost assigned to years prior to either the inception of the plan or subsequent changes in the plan). The choice of number of years is an arbitrary one, although Opinion No. 8 prescribes that it must be between 10 and 40 years. The period most commonly used by the firms visited was 30 years.

The point to be emphasized is that ultimate cost of any changes in a pension plan is independent of acturial assumptions, accounting methods and amortization period. A change in any one of these will change the reported pension expense, and perhaps the annual cash contribution to the fund, but not the eventual amounts of benefits paid. It is easy to confuse increases in pension expense attributable to changes in arbitrarily selected variables with those attributable to substantive changes in the plan. To stress this point, one manager of labor relations recounted how his firm changed certain of its actuarial assumptions and thereby greatly reduced both its annual pension accrual and its cash contribution. The union representative was convinced that the firm had thereby reduced the value of the plan to its employees. The confusion between the changes in amounts to be funded and amounts to be eventually paid in benefits was eliminated only after lengthy explanations.

Industrial relations personnel have no choice but to rely on cost estimates given to them by their consulting actuaries—they are the experts. But it is clear that they must have a thorough understanding of the bases of those estimates if costly errors during contract talks are to be avoided.

Accident and Sickness Insurance

The problems associated with accident and sickness insurance plans are similar to those associated with pension plans. As with pension plans, firms must rely primarily on outside actuarial experts for estimates of costs.

Contracts of most major corporations provide that workers shall receive financial assistance in the event of medical disability. The costs of accident and health insurance are becoming an increasingly large proportion of total labor costs, and, because of rapidly rising medical costs, the trend is likely to continue. Several executives, in fact, when asked to cite the most costly errors they had made in evaluating contract changes, described mistakes involving accident and health insurance plans.

The degree of uncertainty attached to the cost of a medical insurance plan depends largely upon the relationship, if any, between the firm and the insurer. Some companies, for example, contribute a preestablished amount to any legitimate insurance plan of each employee's choosing. Hence, the firm's insurance costs are reasonably fixed and certain, varying only according to the number of employees who elect not to join a plan. Other firms provide insurance coverage directly. Of these the great majority maintain their plans with private insurers, but a few "self-insure" all or a portion of their coverage. To the firms that provide insurance coverage directly, the cost of insurance over the life of the labor contract is uncertain and depends in large measure on the benefits that their employees will actually receive. Each of these firms bears, albeit indirectly, at least a portion of the insurer's risk. For some firms, the outside insurance company is nothing more than an administrator of the plan. Their plans are on a cost-plus basis, with the firms reimbursing the insurance companies for all benefits paid. For other firms the insurance companies pay all claims themselves, but adjust either current or future premiums to reflect company experience; hence over a number of years the costs to the firms are variable.

Each firm visited, with the exception of one that pays a fixed amount to a plan of each employee's choosing, assigns the task of estimating the cost of changes in sickness and accident plans to either the insurance company which administers the plan or to a consulting actuary. Several industrial relations managers complained that the outside experts have had a poor "track record" in predicting the recent increases in medical costs, but they recognize that they have no choice but to rely upon them. As they do with pensions, each company provides the administrator or actuary with necessary demographic data and receives in return an estimate of costs, expressed in either total dollars or cents per labor hour.

The total dollar cost of sickness and accident insurance is, of course, a function of the level of employment; the greater the number of workers employed, the greater the dollar cost. But the cost may also be a function of other variables, of which most firms are likely to be unaware. For example, one industrial relations manager pointed out that the cost of surgical benefits varies directly with the number of men receiving supplementary unemployment benefits. His belief is that when men are out of work, they take advantage of their idle time to have corrective surgery performed. Unfortunately, the correlation between unemployment benefits and hernia operations has not yet been demonstrated to be sufficiently strong that the firm can rely upon it as a basis for estimating insurance costs.

Supplemental Unemployment Benefits (SUB)

TABLE 4.1

SUMMARY OF PROCEDURES USED TO DETERMINE ANNUAL COST OF CHANGES IN SUPPLEMENTAL UNEMPLOYMENT BENEFIT PLANS

No. of Firms [1]	Procedure
4	Assume that maximum possible cents-per-hour contribution to fund will be actual required contribution. Multiply increase in cents-per-hour contribution by number of labor hours in previous year.
1	Uses specially developed model to estimate cost. Model is based on a seven-year period, which includes five "average" years, one "very good" year, and one "very bad" year.

[1] Five firms do not have an income protection plan. One firm has a plan which does not require funding. Instead the firm guarantees to pay employees up to 16 weeks' wages if they are laid off. It bases all cost computations on prior years' experience with the plan.

Although plans designed to provide workers with financial protection against layoffs were adopted by major corporations as early as 1923 (e.g., Procter and Gamble, 1923; George A. Hormel & Company, 1931; Nunn-Bush Shoe Company, 1932), income security plans were seldom negotiated at the bargaining table until the 1950s. In the mid-1950s both the United Automobile Workers and the United Steelworkers made income protection plans their key bargaining demand, and by June 1955 a major automobile manufacturer had agreed to provide its workers with supplemental unemployment benefits (SUB). Since then, SUB plans have been adopted in several major industries.

Although several types of plans are in operation in the firms studied, most follow a basic pattern. The firm makes a cents-per-hour contribution to a special fund until the fund reaches an agreed-upon level. That level is usually expressed in terms of dollars per employee covered. When workers are unemployed, they receive payments from the fund, the amounts of which depend upon the level of the fund.

The plan of one firm visited is reasonably typical of those of the others. Under the terms of the agreement, the company pays into the fund seven cents for each paid labor hour until the total market value of the fund reaches $260 per employee. Thereafter, it contributes lesser amounts (six cents or five cents) until the fund reaches maximum funding of $375 per employee. The right of each employee to draw upon the fund is contingent upon his having accumulated in the fund a sufficient number of "credit units." An employee receives one-half credit unit for each work week in which he receives any compensation, other than SUB, from the company. The maximum number of credit units he may accumulate is a function of his years of service with the company. If he has less than five years of service, the maximum units he may accumulate is 52; if he has between five and 10 years, the maximum is 78; if he has over 25, the maximum is 208. When an employee is either laid off or required to work a reduced number of hours during the week, he is ordinarily eligible to receive benefits. The amount he will receive will be that amount which, when added to any other compensation he may receive from the company and to any state unemployment benefits he may receive, will bring his compensation up to 80 percent of his weekly straight-time pay. For each payment that he receives, a number of credit units will be cancelled, the specific number depending upon his length of service with the firm and the existing level of the fund. For example, if the fund is at 80 percent of maximum, an employee with one to five years' service would lose 1.0 credits for each payment received; if the fund is at between 10.0 and 19.9 percent of maximum, the same employee would lose 5.0 credits for each payment received. An employee with over 20 years of service would lose the same 1.0 credit if the fund is over 80 percent of maximum, but only 1.5 credits if the fund is at between 10.0 and 19.9 percent of maximum.

With only one exception, the firms interviewed consider the annual cost of the plan to be their maximum contribution to the plan. That is, they assume that the fund will never get above the level up to which they must make the greatest cents-per-hour contribution. The firms do not give consideration to probable numbers and patterns of layoffs over the life of the contract. One manager interviewed defended his assumption of the worst possible state of nature on the ground of conservatism. He would rather overestimate that underestimate the cost of the plan. Another, however, indicated that in past years his firm had been operating at considerably reduced levels, so that the fund was sufficiently depleted to make it unlikely that it would be fully funded within the next several years.

Over the long run, that is, several contracts, the assumption of pessimism may be justified for most firms; they may seldom be able to reduce their contributions below the maximum. This is because whenever a company has an opportunity to decrease its cents-per-hour commitment, its union is likely to seek liberalized benefits which will require that contributions be maintained at their previous level.

One firm is considerably more sophisticated than the others in its estimates of SUB costs. The firm uses a special model to determine its probable contribution to its SUB fund. The model is based on what the firm considers an "average" year—an average of the last five years plus a "very good" year and a "very bad" year. The firm assumes that the average year will last for the length of the contract under consideration. The model takes into account the level of employment, the number of workers who receive benefits, the average length of their layoffs and the amount of benefits that they would receive. The model indicates the level of the fund during each month of the contract and the required company contributions.

JOB CLASSIFICATIONS, INEQUITY FUNDS AND
MISCELLANEOUS CONTRACT PROVISIONS

An important and chronic source of controversy between labor and management is how particular jobs should be classified and at what rates, within the agreed-upon wage structure, they should be compensated. The question of the grade to which a job should be assigned clearly has important economic implications. Equally important, however, errors in job classification can have severe impact on worker morale and productivity if employees feel that they are performing either more strenuous or more skilled tasks than other workers who are getting paid more than they. Disputes over job classification are especially likely to arise in periods of rapid technological change when the jobs themselves are continually changing.

Job classification has long been recognized as a legitimate issue for collective bargaining. In all firms visited, classification problems are, for the most part, negotiated at the local level—where both labor and management are most familiar with the specifics of the jobs in question. In some firms, however, classification problems are occasionally brought to the national (or divisional) bargaining tables. When they are, the firms take one of two approaches in evaluating changes in job classifications that are proposed. Under one approach the firm does not attempt to determine the cost of any changes; it treats them as administrative, rather than economic, issues. Under the other approach, changes are handled as are increases in direct wages. The firm determines the total number of labor-hours affected and computes the cost by multiplying the number of labor-hours by the differential in rates between the new and the old job classifications.

Some companies have established formal procedures for reaching agreement on equitable job classifications. Incorporated into the contracts of major steel firms, for example, is a "Job Description and Classification Manual," which prescribes steps to be taken in classifying all new and changed jobs.

A few firms have established "inequity funds" designed to provide additional compensation to employees whose jobs are underrated. Such firms agree to make a cents-per-labor-hour contribution to a special fund. The disposition of the funds either is left entirely to the union or is handled jointly by labor and management. Each of the firms considers the cost of maintaining the fund to be its estimated annual contribution.

The long-range financial burden of an inequity fund, however, is unlikely to be merely the required contributions. For when the fund is used to alleviate an inequity, it is almost certain that the additional cents per hour paid will be built into the base wage of that job at the next bargaining session. Thus, the fund can be used selectively by labor to increase base-wage rates of certain jobs. Moreover, the elimination of one inequity is likely to lead to the creation of another. Workers performing jobs similar to the ones being upgraded are likely to believe that they, too, have been underpaid and are entitled to comparable increases. The financial consequences of establishing an inequity fund may not therefore be obvious; the long-run cost is likely to be considered greater than the cents-per-hour contribution.

"NONECONOMIC" PROVISIONS

Virtually all bargaining agreements contain provisions pertaining to numerous incidental matters, many of which appear to have little economic significance. Many such provisions are policy statements on issues which are usually dealt with at the local level.

Sometimes, however, a change in policy regarding what appears to be a noneconomic matter has important indirect financial implications. Consider, for example, provisions pertaining to work assignments—a matter considered "noneconomic" by many firms. To the extent that a worker is permitted, perhaps by seniority, to have his choice of job assignment, the flexibility of management is limited. It cannot assign a better qualified, though perhaps junior, employee to a job requested by a senior worker. The efficiency of the firm is thereby reduced. Industrial relations officials of all firms interviewed, however, said that unless a proposed work rule change is extraordinary, they do not attempt to determine its cost. They think it is impracticable to do so.

In some firms, because of the nature of operations, changes in provisions pertaining to work assignments have an obvious and direct financial impact. For example, in the airline industry, one component of a pilot's pay is based on seniority. Hence, any proposal which would involve the substitution of a senior pilot for a junior pilot would result in a direct increase in costs. The airline interviewed determines such costs by multiplying its estimates of the number of hours that would be affected by the differential in flight pay.

Many contracts contain detailed provisions relating to the administration of contracts, especially procedures to be followed when an employee files a grievance. No firm at which interviews were conducted attempts to determine the financial impact of changes in administrative provisions (except for one firm which is required to contribute to a special fund to pay workers for time lost when they attend grievance hearings). Some officials observed that such costs were trivial in relation to overall labor costs, and, although attempts are made during the contract period to control them, they are not of concern at the bargaining table.

The important point to be kept in mind is that seemingly non-economic provisions can, in fact, have significant financial consequences. Management should exercise considerable caution before dismissing as immaterial the cost of changes in such provisions.

ECONOMIC VARIABLES

Production Volume and Prices

Both selling prices and production volume are likely to be functions of labor costs. Hence, the impact on profits of a new labor contract will stem not only from changes in direct wages but from accompanying changes in prices and volume as well. On the most obvious level, if the production volume of a firm increases, its total labor costs will almost always increase also. And a firm often responds to increases in wage rates by increasing prices. But relationships among prices, volume and labor costs are seldom so simple; they are often not readily discernible and may sometimes appear contradictory. When a firm increases wages, per-unit labor costs will generally increase. The firm may attempt to maintain previous gross margins by increasing prices, but customers may respond to price increases by reducing their demand for the firm's products.

The severity of customer reaction will depend, of course, on the characteristics of demand: the greater its elasticity, the more pronounced will be the response to price changes. Hence, the firm may have to reduce production volume, and if possible it will reduce the amount of labor employed. Thus, as a result of a new contract, per-unit labor costs and prices may increase, but total labor costs and sales revenues may decline. The problem that the firm faces in assessing the effect of a proposed contract is that of determining the direction and magnitude of such changes in both overall and per-unit costs and revenues.

Production Volume

Of the firms at which interviews were conducted, only one firm—the one which uses the "estimated planning volume"—expressly considers projected volume in determining the financial impact of contract changes. In some firms industrial relations and finance managers, as well as senior executives, receive periodic reports of long-range corporate plans. In evaluating the wage offers that their firms can "afford," they subjectively take into account forecasts of volume. And some officials who compute contract costs on the basis of historical labor requirements compare planned volume with past volume to make certain there are no substantial differences between the two. But in only one firm do analysts actually compute the dollar cost of contract changes using projected, rather than historical, production volume.

Officials interviewed gave several reasons for not expressly taking planned volume into account:

1. Hourly labor costs are more significant in making contract decisions than are overall dollar costs.

2. Most labor costs vary directly with production volume; regardless of volume, labor costs per unit will remain constant. Or, alternatively, labor costs are generally fixed, and total (as opposed to unit) labor costs do not vary with volume.

3. Estimates of future volume are too subjective to be incorporated into cost estimates.

Are such explanations valid? Perhaps, but to a limited extent, at best.

1. Several managers indicated that their objective in bargaining is to minimize the cents-per-hour costs of a settlement and that they give only peripheral regard to the overall effect on profits. Negotiations are conducted, and their success is measured, they pointed out, in terms of cents per hour. If the primary goal of the firm, however, is to increase total dollar profits then the goals of the labor negotiators may, at times, be in conflict with those of the company. The cents-per-productive-hour cost of a benefit (such as an increase in overtime compensation) may be considerably higher at projected levels of production volume, if more overtime will be required, than at the lower historical levels.

2. The variability of labor costs depends upon a firm's production process and its employment policies. The director of industrial relations of a major tire manufacturer observed that in his industry the number of workers assigned to perform functions generally categorized as "overhead" is relatively small and hence labor costs are variable. If the company expands output, it hires new workers rather than operate on an overtime basis. Its labor costs per hour, therefore, remain relatively constant. Managers of chemical, glass and oil firms on the other hand, indicated that in their firms the number of men required to maintain a production process is fixed, regardless of volume. Future amounts of labor used can safely be estimated on the basis of experience. Given the diverse range of activities engaged in by most major corporations, it is often simplistic to say, "our costs are fixed," or "our costs are variable." Most managers are likely to find that the costs of employing certain categories of workers are fixed, whereas those of employing other categories are variable. Thus, in order to determine the impact on profits of a contract change, it is essential to understand how the particular firm's labor costs respond to changes in volume.

3. Although several managers claimed that volume could not be forecast with meaningful precision, they acknowledged that such estimates do, in fact, form the basis of plans in other corporate divisions. An executive of an airline, for example, calculates the cost of contract changes by assuming that current levels of operations will prevail in the future. Yet he admitted that most other major decisions within his firm, such as those pertaining to equipment purchases, are based on anticipated volume, i.e., expected revenue miles flown.

Prices

Not a single firm specifically includes in its analysis price adjustments that it would make in response to increases in labor costs. The one firm which bases cost calculations on anticipated volume uses expected prices to develop an overall corporate plan, and in forecasting prices for the plan anticipated labor-cost increases are among the several factors that are considered. But the firm's model is not circular. Once the estimates of future prices have been made, they are not adjusted in response to proposed contract changes. A financial analyst suggested that although a circular approach might be desirable "in theory," prices, "in practice," are not so sensitive to labor costs that they would be affected by minor differences between actual wage increases and those that were anticipated when the corporate plan was developed.

Managers of other firms gave similar explanations for not considering price adjustments. The vice president of an airline pointed out that fares are established by the Civil Aeronautics Board and are uniform for all carriers along the same routes. Although over a number of years fares may vary with costs, the relationship between fare increases and cost increases attributable to a specific agreement is far too remote to be incorporated into an analysis of that agreement. The industrial relations manager of a chemical company observed that chemical prices are sufficiently competitive that an individual firm is unable to pass on wage increases to its customers. An executive of a meatpacking company noted that the prices of packaged meats are responsive primarily to beef prices; labor costs are relatively unimportant. And the director of industrial relations of an oil company said that wages have but an incidental influence on petroleum prices.

The vice president of finance of an auto supplier commented that one might expect that in his industry it should be possible to pass wage increases on to customers, since the customers are the auto companies—the companies which establish the pattern, which the suppliers must follow, for wage settlements. Nevertheless, he said, the auto companies may have to absorb a portion of their own wage increases, and if they have to do so, they expect their suppliers to do so also. He indicated that because of the difficulty in estimating how much of a price increase the auto firms will actually accept, it would be unproductive to consider potential price increases explicitly when evaluating contract changes.

In some situations, however, the relationship between increases in labor costs and increases in prices may be direct, and can easily be taken into account. Under cost-plus-fixed-fee contracts, or similar cost-oriented agreements, all or a portion of wage increases may be passed on to the purchaser.

Product Mix

A firm might be able to minimize the adverse effect on profits of a wage increase by changing its product mix. If a firm produces more than one product, it is improbable that a contract settlement will cause the labor costs of each of several products to increase by equal proportions relative to other costs. The ratios of labor to materials and labor to capital are likely to be different. An increase in wages might, therefore, make some products comparatively less profitable than it would make others. To maximize profits, assuming constraints on available resources, the firm would have to shift productive resources from the relatively less profitable to the relatively more profitable products, and it might have to change the size and skill composition of its work force.

No firm, however, gives specific consideration to potential changes in product mix. Officials interviewed maintained that such changes are difficult to forecast and, when made, cannot often be traced to a specific cause, such as a contract settlement.

But some industrial relations officials noted that they are cognizant of possible adjustments and often make their union counterparts aware of them. An executive of a firm in which one product accounts for a large percentage of its sales revenue pointed out that any wage increase it negotiates is usually matched by its competitors. But the company also produces several miscellaneous products in competition with many small operators, some of whom are not unionized and pay considerably lower wages. The firm is not likely to be able to increase prices on the miscellaneous products and they will therefore decline in profitability—some to the extent that they must be abandoned. The company threatens the union with plant closings, but it nevertheless does not incorporate the portended changes into its own cost calculations.

Another manager offered this example of why he finds it useful to be advised of possible plant closings resulting from changes in product mix: In negotiating job security provisions the firm is sometimes able to trade off increases in benefits for workers who have been laid off with those for employees who are on a "short" workweek. If he is aware of pending plant closings, he can attempt to shift union demands from increases in the former benefits to increases in the latter.

Capital Investments and Technological Improvements

The financial outcomes of contract changes are functions of both size and skill composition of a firm's labor force. To determine the ultimate influence of wage increases on profits, the firm must, therefore, be aware of any anticipated changes in plant and equipment and also of opportunities to reduce the burden of higher labor costs by substituting capital for labor.

To maximize total output, a firm should employ each of its resources up to the point at which the marginal physical product of a dollar's worth of one resource is equal to the marginal physical product of a dollar's worth of every other resource. If a firm had been operating under its old contract with the optimum proportion of labor to capital, an increase in labor costs relative to capital costs should induce it to increase its use of capital relative to labor. In practice, upon signing a new contract, a firm might review proposed capital projects. Presumably, projects which previously had been near the margin might, if their costs remained stable, be accepted when reevaluated in the light of the increase in labor costs. To the extent that such projects are, in fact, accepted, the amount of labor used can be reduced.

Nevertheless, of the 11 firms studied, only two take into account planned changes in plant and equipment. One firm, again the one which bases calculations on the "estimated planning volume," determines its labor requirements only after making allowance for planned capital expansion. For example, if the firm plans to shift a portion of its operations from an old plant to a new one which will require less labor per unit of output than the old, the analyst determines the cost of contract changes using the estimated number of labor-hours at the new, rather than the old, plant. The other firm, an airline, cannot avoid paying attention to the planned introduction of new equipment, since the wages of pilots (hourly pay, gross weight pay and mileage pay, in particular) depend upon type of equipment flown. Once the rates for a new aircraft have been agreed upon, however, the firm assumes, when negotiating subsequent contracts, that the composition of its fleet will remain unchanged.

Not one company visited, according to officials responsible for contract analysis, reevaluates capital expenditure proposals to determine whether previously rejected projects should now be accepted. The most frequently cited reason for not doing so was that labor costs have but a minor influence on decisions to construct new facilities or purchase new equipment. Industrial relations managers of firms in the chemical and oil industries, both of which are capital-intensive, maintained that labor costs are, in fact, a negligible factor in capital decisions.

Several labor relations officials noted that there is little exchange of information between departments involved in labor negotiations and those concerned with capital improvements. They observed that the industrial relations department sometimes is asked to provide the budgeting department with estimates of future wage rates, and they believe that such estimates are sufficiently accurate to be used for capital expenditure analysis. But there is little communication between departments relating specifically to collective bargaining.

"SPILLOVER"

TABLE 4.2

SUMMARY OF EXTENT TO WHICH FIRMS CONSIDER EFFECT OF "SPILLOVER"

No. of Firms	Extent of Consideration
1	Gives no consideration.
3	Recognize that increases will have to be given to exempt employees, but do not explicitly compute cost of such increases.
6	Make "rough" estimate of cost of increases to be given to exempt employees. Usually assume that exempt employees will be given same percentage increases as provided for in contract.
1	Makes detailed estimate of cost of increases. Assumes that exempt employees will be given same percentage increases as provided for in contract. Takes into account impact of both "roll-up" and "package roll-up."

Once it has reached agreement with its labor unions, a firm is likely to find that it must automatically grant to nonunion employees certain of the increases in wages and benefits that it is committed to give to union employees. For example, if a company accedes to a union demand for an additional holiday and intends to close its plants on that day, nonunion employees may also have to be given the day off. If all employees are included in the same accident and sickness insurance plan, nonunion as well as union employees will have to receive the benefits of an increase in coverage. Other increases in compensation may be granted as a matter of policy. Some firms, for instance, traditionally increase the wages of nonunion employees by the same percentage as they have agreed to increase those of union employees.

Only one firm makes detailed estimates of the financial burden of "spillover." It assumes that employees who are exempt from provisions of the labor contract will be granted the same percentage wage increases and similar improvements in benefits as employees who are covered. The firm estimates directly the cost of the wage and benefit increases and computes and adds to such cost provisions for "roll-up" and "package roll-up." Six other firms estimate the potential consequences of "spillover" by determining the percentage by which the total compensation of covered employees will increase and applying that percentage to the current annual compensation of exempt employees. The remaining firms do not even quantify the cost of probable wage and salary increases to nonunion employees.

POST-CONTRACT AUDITS

Although many firms spend considerable time in determining the cost of contract changes, most never evaluate, either during or at the expiration of the contract, the accuracy of their estimates. Of the firms at which interviews were conducted, only two review their original computations. One of the two reviews the original estimates of specific contract changes on an *ad hoc* basis. The other prepares formal statements reconciling actual with estimated costs.

One industrial relations manager minimized the value of a post-contract audit, commenting that "there are just too many variables which determine the eventual cost of a contract" (although the very purpose of such an audit is to assist management in identifying such variables). Another manager noted that labor costs are included in a corporate profit plan, for which a reconciliation of actual and budgeted amounts is prepared. But, he admitted, the reconciliation is not intended to isolate variances attributable to errors in contract evaluation, and the labor cost figures are in insufficient detail to permit recognition of mistakes pertaining to specific provisions.

The financial analyst who prepares the formal reconciliation indicated that over a number of contracts the differences between actual and estimated costs has been surprisingly small. What errors there have been have been the result primarily of incorrect assumptions of volume, labor mix, medical costs and the behavior of the consumer price index.

SUMMARY

The majority of firms examine the financial consequences of changes in contract terms on the basis of past, rather than future, manpower requirements. They disregard their capabilities to lessen, by modifying previously developed corporate plans, the burden of increases in compensation, and they neglect to evaluate all but the most direct effects of contract revisions. Most firms make no provision in their analyses for potential adjustments, attributable to contract revisions, in product and labor-rate mixes, and they ignore intended openings of new plants or planned introduction of labor-saving equipment. Their analyses emphasize the cost, rather than the effect on profits, of proposed settlements.

The consequences of evaluating contract revisions from a historical rather than a future perspective, and of ignoring the indirect implications of the changes, is evident in the analyses accorded specific provisions—e.g., those pertaining to direct wage rates and compensated time off. All of the firms that compute the cents-per-hour cost of a direct wage increase determine a "roll-up" percentage to reflect the additional costs that the firm will incur as a result of having to increase those benefits which are dependent upon base wage rates. But only two firms recompute the percentage to take into account modifications in the benefits themselves that might be negotiated concurrently with wage increases. The other firms are likely to underestimate the cost of the wage increases by failing to foresee the increase in benefit costs attributable to the increase in wages.

In assessing the cost of additional time off with pay (e.g., holidays, vacations, relief time), many firms estimate, on the basis of previous experience, only the accounts that will actually be charged to specific labor-cost accounts. They neglect to consider the effect on profits of the services lost: how much production will be sacrificed; how such production will be recovered. These firms are unlikely, therefore, to be aware of the overall impact of the increased compensation by reason of modifications of time-off provisions.

One company is an exception. It is characteristically oriented toward the future rather than the past and toward profits rather than costs. This firm employs its "estimated planning volume" as the foundation for its analyses, and thus the burden of increases in wages or benefits is calculated by using estimates of hours to be worked in years covered by the agreement currently being negotiated, not historical records of hours worked during the contract which is about to expire. Plans for changes in labor-rate, labor-capital and product mixes are an integral part of its evaluation.

The far-reaching approach taken by this company is manifest in its review of particular provisions. In estimating the cost of an additional holiday, for example, a financial analyst first establishes, on the basis of the estimated planning volume, the number of units initially scheduled for the particular day. He then examines the alternatives for rescheduling such production at other times and assesses the resultant additional labor costs. Similarly, in forecasting the cost of extra relief time the analyst computes not the wages to be paid to the men on relief (who would have to be compensated anyway), but rather those to be paid to their substitutes.

In evaluating the impact of "roll-up" the firm takes into account increases in benefits negotiated concurrently with those in direct wages. It is the only one visited that makes detailed estimates of the effects of "spillover" and which conducts comprehensive post-contract audits.

The firm accounts for probable increases in labor costs when determining optimum "economic variables," such as price, volume, product mix and capital-labor mix, although it does not explicitly consider, as part of its evaluation of contract proposals, potential modifications of the variables. In the past, differences between the forecast increases in compensation and those actually negotiated have not been sufficiently great to necessitate change in original plans. Other companies, however, neglect to consider not only potential adjustments in the economic variables that they may make as a result of changes in labor costs, but the effect on labor costs of revisions in the economic variables that were planned independently of the outcome of the labor negotiations as well.

Like most others, the firm reduces the cost of all increases to a single cents-per-hour figure. But the expression does not suffer from the major weaknesses of those calculated by the other firms. It represents total compensation costs divided by estimated man-hours of labor, but included in total compensation costs are indirect, as well as direct, outlays. Unlike the "traditional" cents-per-hour expressions, it does in fact incorporate consideration of company plans for the future, and it does take into account the opportunity cost of reduced production.

Table 4.3 compares evaluation procedures that are distinctively past-oriented with those that are future-oriented. Characteristic of the past procedures is that they employ historical accounting information. Each of the past-directed techniques requires information as to either the number of hours worked, or the amount of compensation charged to particular labor-cost accounts, in prior years. By contrast, common to all of the future-directed procedures is that they are based upon estimates of hours worked or amounts to be paid during the period covered by the new contract, rather than that which is about to expire.

In all firms studied, the projections that would be required if the future-oriented methods were to be employed are currently made and incorporated into decisions involving problems other than collective bargaining. In some firms such forecasts are presently supplied to, although not used by, industrial relations executives, and in at least one firm the projections are furnished even to union negotiators!

In the one exceptional firm, corporate plans are prepared in far greater detail than in the other firms visited. Projections of volume, for example, are broken down by product, by month and by plant, and on the basis of such forecasts relatively precise estimates are made of the required number of man-hours and the mix of rates at which they will be compensated. But the procedures followed by the other firms are deficient as compared with those of the unusual firm, not because the firms use data that are in insufficient detail but because they use the *wrong* data. They use historical instead of projected data. And they do so despite the availability of the projected data.

TABLE 4.3

COMPARISON OF EVALUATION PROCEDURES THAT ARE PAST-ORIENTED
WITH THOSE THAT ARE FUTURE-ORIENTED

Issue	Past-Oriented Procedure	Future-Oriented Procedure
Direct wages	Negotiated cents per hour multiplied by number of productive hours in prior year.	Negotiated costs per hour multiplied by anticipated number of productive hours.
Effect of increase in direct wages on fringe benefits	"Roll-up" percentage is based entirely on prior year's experience and provisions of contract which is about to expire.	"Roll-up" percentage takes into account increases in benefits being negotiated concurrently with increases in wages.
Overtime premiums and shift differentials	Increase in rates is multiplied by number of hours paid at premium rates in prior years.	Increase in rates is multiplied by number of hours paid at premium rates that will be required by anticipated production volume.
Cost-of-living adjustments	Cost is determined in same manner as other direct wage increases. Assumption is made that maximum wage increase possible will be actual increase that firm is required to grant.	Cost is determined in same manner as other direct wage increases. Estimates of cents-per-hour rates are based on explicit forecasts of behavior of appropriate price index.
Vacations	Either number of additional vacation hours is multiplied by base wage rates, or number of additional vacation hours is multiplied by amounts charged to vacation accounts in past year and divided by number of productive hours in past year.	Estimates are made of amount of lost production attributable to additional vacation days and of number of workers who will have to be replaced, who will have to work overtime at time and one-half the base wage rate, and who will have to work overtime at twice the base wage rate in order to fulfill production requirements. Number of additional hours for which employees will have to be compensated is multiplied by appropriate rates.

TABLE 4.3—Contd.

Issue	Past-Oriented Procedure	Future-Oriented Procedure
Holidays	Either number of additional holiday hours is multiplied by appropriate base wage rates, or amounts charged to holiday pay account in previous year are multiplied by appropriate percentage.	Estimates are made of amount of lost production attributable to additional holiday hours and number of man-hours at straight-time and premium rates that will be required to recover lost production. Numbers of hours are multiplied by appropriate rates. To total wages is added costs of capital required to expand physical facilities.
Relief time	Total hours of additional relief time are multiplied by appropriate base wage rates.	Special relief-time formula is used. Formula determines number of additional employees who would have to be hired.
Pensions and accident and health insurance	—	Requisite demographic data are given to consulting actuaries. Computations are necessarily future-oriented since techniques employed by actuaries are based on estimates of such variables as turnover, interest to be earned on pension funds, mortality rates, and hospital costs.
Supplemental unemployment benefits	Cost is based on assumption that maximum possible cents-per-hour contribution to fund will be the actual required contribution. Increase in cents-per-hour contribution is multiplied by number of men employed in previous year.	Specially developed model is used to study probable behavior of SUB fund. Model is based on probabilities of alternative states of nature (e.g., good year, bad year, average year). Takes into account projected levels of employment and required benefit payments given each state of nature.

The discounted cash flow model is one means of assuring that contract evaluations are made with a view toward the future rather than the past. The model is a technique whereby all incremental cash flows associated with an expenditure proposal are identified and discounted back to the present. It explicitly requires that anticipated, not past, cash outlays be assessed. A principal advantage of the model is that it permits the firm to take into account increases in revenues, as well as expenses, and thereby to determine the impact of contract changes on profits instead of only costs. Furthermore, the model enables the firm to add another dimension—the time value of money—to its review of contract proposals.

CHAPTER V

The Discounted Cash Flow Model

ADVANTAGES OF THE MODEL

The discounted cash flow model is a widely used management technique to evaluate long-range expenditure proposals. The model focuses on the cash receipts and disbursements associated with a proposal and explicitly and automatically weighs the time value of money. The model requires that a manager identify the cash inflows and outflows associated with a proposal and discount them back to the present (i.e., adjust the flows to take into account interest that is gained or lost because cash is to be paid or received in the future rather than at present). Other things being equal, the manager would select the proposal requiring the smallest *discounted* cash outflow or largest *discounted* cash inflow.

In order to employ the discounted cash flow model to evaluate labor contract proposals, a manager would first determine the incremental cash flows that would arise from each of the alternatives under consideration. He would consider not only the direct receipts and disbursements associated with the contract changes, but also cash flows in all phases of the firm's operations that would be affected if the proposals were to be accepted. He would explicitly recognize changes in price, volume, product mix and labor-capital mix, as well as any other changes that the firm previously had planned or would be likely to make in the future in an attempt to minimize the adverse consequences of the new contract. Using an "internal rate of return" or a rate of interest that is appropriate for his particular company, he would find the present value of, or "discount" back to the present, all anticipated inflows and outflows. Other things being equal, he would prefer those contract changes in which the present value of the net outflows was the smallest.

The discounted cash flow model, while most often used to appraise capital investment projects, can be used to evaluate any expenditure that requires a commitment of resources for which the associated benefits and costs can be expected to be realized over a reasonably long period of time. Labor contracts require such a commitment. The firm promises to compensate employees at an established rate over the life of the contract in return for their services.

The model is especially useful for selecting among alternatives with differing cash flows which must be reduced to a common expression before they can be compared, and contract proposals are often associated with distinctive patterns of receipts and disbursements. For example, a proposal which would grant employees a large increase in the first year of a three-year contract and no additional increase in subsequent years would have a different pattern of outlays than one which would grant smaller increases in each year of the contract. The discounted cash flow model indicates the value of each cash stream in a single, comparable figure—net present value of the cash flow.

The similarities between labor contracts and capital expenditures are sufficiently great to suggest that the discounted cash flow model could be used to assess labor contract proposals as well as capital projects. Both involve long-term commitments and varying patterns of cash flow. In fact, if one accepts a sufficiently broad definition of "capital expenditure," labor contracts might even be considered a type of capital expenditure. One noted management consultant, for example, maintains that "capital expenditure" should be defined in terms of economic behavior (as opposed to acounting convention) and the criterion should be "flexibility of the commitment involved." In making business decisions, he emphasizes, the broader definition is needed even though some investments—he cites cumulative advertising as an example—"cannot be measured neatly either in amount or in productivity."[1] Labor contracts would

---

[1] Joel Dean, CAPITAL BUDGETING (New York: Columbia University Press, 1951), pp. 4-5.

clearly fall within the scope of the broader definition. Unlike many conventional investments, which entail one or more periods of cash outlays followed by one or more periods of cash receipts, labor contracts generally involve cash outlays over the life of the contract and cash receipts which cannot necessarily be attributed directly to the outlays. But the distinction is not critical. Many capital expenditures are associated with patterns of cash flow in which the relationship between receipts and disbursements is not readily discernible, but as long as incremental cash flows can be ascribed to one alternative rather than to another, the investment decision can be implemented by the discounted cash flow model.

The discounted cash flow model exhibits several characteristics which make it especially attractive for effecting labor contract decisions. Among them are:

1. The model specifically takes into account the time value of money.

2. The model provides a frame of reference for a thorough and systematic analysis of the financial impact of a proposal. It enables management to take into account operational changes that the firm is likely to make in order to adjust to the new contract.

3. The information returned by the model is easy to understand, and since the model summarizes the value of a proposal in a single figure, it facilitates comparisons among alternative proposals.

4. The model avoids problems of allocations inherent in evaluation techniques based on "accounting" income.

1. *The model explicitly takes into account the time value of money.* A dollar saved today is worth much more than a dollar earned tomorrow. The dollar saved today, if invested in corporate assets, will appreciate in value with the passage of time. If a company is able to earn a return on invested capital of 10 percent per year, the dollar received today is the equivalent of $1.10 received a year from now or, assuming that the "interest" is reinvested, $1.21 two years from now. To put it another way, the "present value" or "discounted value" of $1.21 to be received two years hence is, assuming a "discount rate" of 10 percent, $1.00. The present value of $1 to be received 10 years from now is only $.386.

Insofar as most labor contracts are for periods of three years or less, the time value of money is not as significant as it would be if the contract extended over longer periods of time. But it may be of sufficient importance that it cannot be ignored. For many firms the "cost of capital" or the required rate of return on invested capital is over 10 percent; hence, the difference in value between cash flow in absolute dollars and in discounted dollars is likely to be substantial, even over a three-year period. A wage increase granted early in the contract period is obviously more costly than one granted later in the period since the former extends over a longer period of time and, therefore, requires the expenditure of a greater number of absolute dollars. But how much more costly is it? It is more costly to the extent that the present value of the dollars paid over the longer period is greater than the present value of the dollars paid over the shorter period. And the difference in cost between the two increases may be significantly greater (because of the greater weight given to dollars disbursed in the near, instead of the distant, future) when expressed in terms of discounted dollars than in absolute dollars.

Some contract changes, however, commit the firm to a series of cash outlays over a considerably greater number of years than the contract period itself. In such cases it is imperative that the time value of money be taken into account. Dollars to be disbursed in the distant future are of considerably less value than dollars to be disbursed in the more immediate future. A pension plan which requires funding only after several years, for example, can be compared to a benefit requiring immediate cash outlays only when the two are expressed in common, i.e., discounted dollar, terms.

In addition, it is necessary to consider the impact of a current wage agreement on future contract settlements. A wage increase granted at any time during a present contract will be incorporated into the wage rate on which future increases will be based. But since the cost of such increases will not be incurred until the relatively distant future, they can be evaluated only when costs are expressed in discounted dollar terms.

2. *The model provides a frame of reference for a thorough and systematic analysis of the financial impact of a proposal. It enables management to take into account operational changes that the firm is likely to make in order to adjust to the new contract.*

The extent to which a firm can "afford" a contract settlement is largely a function of the changes it makes in response to it. It is essential, therefore, that management consider the changes it is likely to make before, rather than after, the contract is signed. Although it may be impossible to isolate all changes that the firm will make in response to other factors, the cash flow model encourages management to consider the major changes that it should properly make. The model by no means guarantees that the manager will take into account all relevant adjustments to operations, and it is certainly not the only technique which enables him to consider such adjustments. But the model does provide a framework for the systematic analysis of such changes—an analysis that the firm may not make if it uses the average cents-per-hour techniques illustrated in Chapter I.

Changes in prices, product mix, labor-capital mix and volume are among those that management generally should consider. Suppose, for example, that management is evaluating a proposed increase in wages. Among the many questions it might want to raise are the following:

How much of the increase will it be able to pass on to customers?

What will be the probable operating volume, given the new price structure?

Will certain products have to be dropped because the firm will be unable to compete with firms that do not have to grant the same wage increases? How will the firm utilize the resources previously devoted to such products?

Can the firm reduce the impact of the wage increase by installing labor-saving equipment?

The discounted cash flow model provides an efficient means of explicitly considering such questions and of studying the interaction of the various operational changes the firm is likely to make.

To the extent that the discounted cash flow model leads the manager to a greater understanding of the financial impact of a proposal, it should better enable him to recognize modifications that might make the financial impact less severe. A union is often amenable to such modifications, especially if the firm is willing to grant additional wages or benefits in exchange. The union may be as well satisfied with the contract after the modifications as before, but the cost savings to the firm may be considerable. Similarly, the model may indicate to management alternative wage and benefit packages which are more acceptable to labor yet no more costly to the firm than those which union negotiators have previously rejected.

Relationships between labor costs and other operational variables are especially complex. But merely because it may be difficult to identify all cash receipts and outlays associated with a change in labor costs does not mean that an attempt need not be made. An analysis that recognizes the indirect effects of a change in labor costs would certainly have to be more extensive, and perhaps more costly, than one that does not. But if the investment is a large one, the benefits to be derived from a comprehensive, rather than a superficial, analysis are likely to be substantial.

3. *The information returned by the model is easy to understand, and since the model summarizes the present value of a proposal in a single figure, it facilitates comparisons of alternative proposals.* Once the appropriate cash flows have been identified, the net present value of a contract proposal can be computed using straightforward mechanical techniques. Alternatives can be ranked according to their net present values, and the rankings present no complex problems of interpretation.

By expressing the merits of a labor contract proposal in a single figure which encompasses the receipts and disbursements attributable to a proposal over its entire lifetime, the discounted cash flow model enables the manager to make comparisons that might be misleading if the financial impact of the proposal were expressed in terms of average cents per hour. Traditional cents-per-hour comparisons are likely to be deceiving if they fail to take into account the fixed or variable behavior of the cash flows. The average cents-per-hour cost of a medical plan, for example, cannot properly be compared with that of a base-hourly-rate increase if the number of hours worked is uncertain. An increase in the number of hours worked by a labor force of fixed size over the number of hours on which the average was based might cause no increase in the cash outlays associated with the medical plan, but it would cause a substantial increase in those associated with the direct wages.

4. *The model avoids problems of allocations inherent in evaluation techniques based on "accounting" income.* Only cash, not earnings, can be invested in other capital projects, used to retire debt or distributed to shareholders. The amount of cash received or disbursed can be objectively measured and is not subject to the interperiod allocations, oftentimes arbitrary, that are necessary for the determination of income.

Although most benefits would have an identical effect on both cash flow and earnings, a few would have a substantially different impact on the two. Pension costs, for example, may be charged to income in years other than those in which the corresponding cash is contributed to the pension fund.

ACCEPTANCE OF THE MODEL

The discounted cash flow model, although increasingly being used to evaluate capital projects, has not yet attained complete acceptance. Its failure to do so may be ascribed to certain limitations and difficulties in practice.

1. The model implicitly assumes that the firm has a single goal: to maximize the net present value of a stream of future cash flows. Many firms, though, have as their primary objective the achievement of a stated level of earnings per share, an objective that may be inconsistent with that of maximizing the present value of cash flow. Firms with multiple objectives will get incomplete evaluation from the discounted cash flow model. Nevertheless, in defense of the model it should be observed that it may be used advantageously as long as cash flow is one of the criteria. Furthermore, when reviewing contract proposals the firm is less likely to find the goal of maximizing the present value of cash flow inconsistent with that of its objectives related to profits than when evaluating conventional investment proposals because labor costs are generally charged as expenses in the period in which the cash is disbursed, or in the one immediately following.

2. The model requires that the firm explicitly determine a discount rate. Most firms consider the cost of capital to be the

appropriate rate. Yet the concept of "cost of capital" has, at best, proven elusive, despite a number of research efforts.[2]

3. The model necessitates estimates of future cash flows. Many executives have questioned their ability to generate the required projections, especially for periods beyond the "short run." [3]

There is evidence that firms are becoming more receptive to the model than they were previously. A survey published in 1966 revealed that only a small percentage of firms questioned used the discounted cash flow model to evaluate capital projects.[4] In sharp contrast, however, a similar study in 1971 indicated that over half of the respondents, all large manufacturing concerns, followed discounting procedures.[5] Firms which currently use discounted cash flow techniques could probably apply the model, with little difficulty to the evaluation of labor contracts.

CENTS-PER-HOUR COMPUTATIONS

The discounted cash flow model traditionally has been used to examine the *net cash flows* of the several alternatives under consideration. The common practice in labor negotiations is to evaluate contract proposals by comparing the *cents-per-hour* effects of the proposals. The cents-per-hour form has been used in the discounted cash flow analysis in the remainder of this discussion because it was clear from the inteviews conducted that labor negotiators and managers would prefer to assess contracts in terms of cents-per-hour, rather than total, cost.

In order to gain the advantages of the discounted cash flow approach, it is essential that the cents-per-hour data be used prop-

---

[2] For a discussion of the concept of cost of capital, see Ezra Solomon, THE THEORY OF FINANCIAL MANAGEMENT (New York: Columbia University Press, 1963).

[3] For more complete discussions of the limitations of the discounted cash flow model, see Alexander A. Robichek, Donald G. Ogilvie and John D. C. Roach, *Capital Budgeting: A Pragmatic Approach,* FINANCIAL EXECUTIVE, XXXVII (April, 1969), 26-39; and Eugene M. Lerner and Alfred Rappaport, *Limit DCF in Capital Budgeting,* HARVARD BUSINESS REVIEW, XLVI (September-October, 1968), 133-139.

[4] George A. Christy, CAPITAL BUDGETING: CURRENT PRACTICES AND THEIR EFFICIENCY (Eugene, Oregon: Bureau of Business and Economic Research, University of Oregon, 1966), p. 12.

[5] Thomas P. Klammer, "A Study of the Association of Capital Budgeting Techniques with Firm Performance and Firm Characteristics" (unpublished Ph.D. dissertation, University of Wisconsin, 1971), p. 77.

erly to reflect the future consequences of the contract proposals. Thus, the traditional cents-per-hour figure is inappropriate since it is based exclusively on historical information.

The following pages describe the information needs and the procedures to be followed to arrive at a suitable cents-per-hour cost. The basic characteristic of the required data is that they must represent the labor input of future activities and must recognize the interrelationships between labor costs and other aspects of the firm's operations.

Cents-per-hour cost represents:

Net Cash Effect of Contract Proposals
Given Projected Operating Response

———————————————

Anticipated Productive Hours

Outlined below are factors to be considered in determining both numerator and denominator:

I. *Net Cash Effect of Contract Proposals and Projected Operating Response*
   A. *Cost of Specific Contract Terms*
      1. *Direct Wages*
         Data required: Proposed wage increase; anticipated number of productive hours.
         Usual sources of data: Anticipated number of productive hours can be derived from estimates of production volume contained in corporate profit plans.
      2. *Effect of Direct Wage Increase on Fringe Benefit Costs*
         Data required: Amounts charged to accounts of fringe benefits whose costs are direct functions of the direct wage rate (e.g., payroll taxes, overtime premiums, payments for time not worked); anticipated projected hours.
         Usual sources of data: Payroll and labor-cost accounts; anticipated productive hours can be derived from estimates of production volume.
         Procedure: Compute "roll-up" and "package roll-up" percentages by following procedures described and illustrated in Chapter III (pages 35-39). Multiply cost of direct wage increases by sum of the two percentages.

3. *Overtime Premiums and Shift Differentials*

Data required: Anticipated number of hours that will be compensated at premium rates.

Usual sources of data: Anticipated number of hours that will be compensated at premium rates can be derived from production schedules and estimates of production volume.

Procedure: Multiply increases in overtime premiums and shift differentials by anticipated number of hours that will be compensated at premium rates. The premium rates should be based on the *old* direct wage rate. Increases in premiums attributable to increases in the direct wage rate will be accounted for in both of the "roll-up" percentages.

4. *Incentive Wages*

Data required: Proposed increase in rates; projected number of incentive units that will be earned.

Usual sources of data: Number of incentive units that will be earned can be derived from estimates of production volume contained in corporate profit plans as well as incentive schedules and records of past employee performance.

Procedure: Multiply increase in rates by projected number of incentive units that will be earned. Account for effect of the increase on cost of fringe benefits by following "roll-up" procedures outlined in Chapter III.

5. *Cost-of-Living Adjustments*

Data required: Estimates of most likely increases in rates; anticipated number of productive hours.

Usual sources of data: Estimates of most likely increases in rates can generally be obtained from company economics department or consulting economists; anticipated number of productive hours can be derived from estimates of production volume contained in corporate profit plans.

Procedure: Multiply increase in rates by anticipated number of productive hours. Account for effect of the increase on cost of fringe benefits by following "roll-up" procedures outlined in Chapter III.

6. *Compensation for Time Not Worked (Including Vacations, Holidays, Relief Time, Jury Duty, Etc.)*

Data required: Forecasts of production that will be lost because of additional time off; estimates of number of hours that will be required to recover lost production; cost of such hours based on old base wage rates; cost of capital required to expand physical plant; estimates of number of new employees who might have to be hired; estimates of costs of hiring and training new employees.

Usual sources of data: Number of units of production lost can be derived from monthly production forecasts and statistics of productivity per man. Estimates of number of hours and rates of pay required to recover lost production can be made by reviewing policies followed by firm in past years. Number of new employees who will have to be hired can be determined by reviewing past practices and, in some cases, by employing special formulas (e.g., the "relief-time formula" described in Chapter III, pages 55-56). Cost of capital required to finance plant expansion can be determined by finance and production departments; costs of hiring and training new employees can be obtained from the personnel department.

Procedure: Multiply number of hours that will be required to recover lost production by rate (based on old contract) at which they will be compensated. Add cost of capital required to expand physical plant and of hiring and training new employees.

The number of hours that will be required to recover lost production must be costed at rates which were applicable under the old contract. The increases in rates in the new contract will be accounted for in the "roll-up" and "package roll-up" percentages.

Cost of hiring and training new personnel should be added to the cost of the contract for only the year in which they will be incurred. Thus, costs of hiring permanent personnel may be incurred only in the first year of the contract; those of hiring temporary personnel may be incurred during each year of the contract.

7. *Pensions and Accident and Health Insurance*

Data required: Demographic statistics on employee population.

Usual sources of data: Personnel files.

Procedure: Estimated total cost of providing benefits should be computed by professional actuaries.

8. *Supplemental Unemployment Benefits*

Data required: Anticipated number of hours on which contributions to fund must be made; required cents-per-hour contribution.

Usual sources of data: Anticipated number of hours on which contribution to fund must be made may sometimes be derived from forecasts of production; other times, however, it can be obtained only from a detailed study of probable behavior of fund.

Procedure: If contract specifies that contribution must be made on all hours of paid compensation until fund reaches a maximum level and such level is unlikely to be reached during the year under consideration, then total cost can be determined by multiplying cents-per-hour contribution by estimated number of hours on which contribution is required. Alternatively, if fund is likely to remain above maximum level without additional funding, then total cost is likely to be zero. If, however, the required contribution is not obvious from the level of the fund and the provisions of the contract, firm may have to develop special model, which incorporates estimates of future rates of layoffs, to study behavior of fund and determine most probable cost.

B. *Other Considerations*

1. *"Spillover"*

Data required: Same types of data as are required to compute cost of increases in wages and benefits for employees covered by contract; projections of which specific wage or benefit increases are likely to be granted to exempt employees.

Usual sources: Projections of which specific wages or benefit increases are likely to be granted exempt employees can ordinarily be made by members of the personnel department who are responsible for formulating wage and salary policies.

Procedure: To compute costs of increases in wages and benefits for exempt employees, follow same procedures (including calculation of "roll-up") as for covered employees.

2. *Changes in "Economic Variables" (Price, Product Mix, Labor-Capital Mix) Made in Response to Contract Changes*

Data required: Estimates of adjustments in economic variables, other than those previously planned, that will be made because of proposed changes in labor costs.

Usual sources: Executives of marketing, production and corporate-planning departments.

Procedures: From either total costs or cost of changes in specific provisions, add or subtract incremental outlays attributable to projected adjustments.

The changes referred to in this section are those which the firm might make in order to maximize profits (or to attain other corporate objectives) and often require revisions in overall corporate plans. They are of the type which are generally considered on an on-going basis and which, as several executives who were interviewed indicated, are not often associated with specific contract modifications. Nevertheless, there are situations when adjustments in the economic variables can, in fact, be traced with relative ease to changes in labor costs. For example, if a firm's prices are strongly cost-oriented, then increases in revenues can be directly attributable to increases in wages. Hence, the added revenues should be deducted from total costs of the contract change.

II. *Anticipated Productive Hours*

Data required: Anticipated production volume.

Usual sources: Corporate profit plans.

Procedures: Determine historic relationships between units produced and number of labor hours used. Adjust for planned changes in product mix and labor-capital mix.

The number of anticipated productive hours must take into account changes in product mix and labor-capital mix that were planned before consideration was given to the contract being negotiated, but it must exclude adjustments attributable to changes in the contract itself. Certain contract changes may induce the firm to increase or decrease the number of productive hours initially scheduled. In order to permit proper comparisons among alternative proposals, however, the base number of hours must remain unchanged. Thus, the incremental receipts or disbursements attributable to the adjustment must be added or subtracted from the total cost of the contract revisions, but the number of productive hours must remain unchanged. For example, the procedures outlined for determining the cost of increases in compensated time off are based on the assumption that the firm will be able (either by scheduling overtime work or by expanding the labor force) to maintain previously scheduled production levels. But should the firm be unable to do so—and thereby be forced to reduce sales volume—the incremental profit on the sales lost must be added to total cost. The number of productive hours used to compute cents-per-hour costs should remain unchanged from that originally scheduled, even though the reduction in production volume will force the firm to reduce its number of productive (but *not* compensated) hours.

Similarly, anticipated productive hours should include only those of employees actually covered by the agreement. In considering the impact of "spillover," for example, outlays necessitated by the extension of wages and benefit increases to exempt employees would be added to costs, but the number of hours which they work would not be included in anticipated productive hours.

III. *Computation of Percentage Increase*

Data required: Cents-per-hour cost of increase; initial cents-per hour cost of wages and benefits.

Usual sources: Initial cents-per-hour wage can be determined from corporate payroll accounts and records of productive hours.

Procedure: Divide cost of increase by cost of initial wages and benefits. In computing percentage increases, the initial cents-per-hour cost of wages and benefits must be calculated in a manner consistent with that used to determine the incremental cost of the revisions. Thus, if the cents-per-hour cost of contract changes takes into account probable increases in wages and benefits that will be granted to exempt employees, then the initial cents-per-hour cost must include the current compensation of such employees. Ordinarily the initial cents-per-hour cost can be computed by dividing total costs of compensating both workers who are covered by the agreement and those exempt employees who are included in the calculation of the increase, by anticipated productive hours.

AN ILLUSTRATION OF CENTS-PER-HOUR COMPUTATIONS

An example of the computation of the cents-per-hour cost of contract changes might be helpful. The illustration will consider only the cost of contract changes in the first year of a multi-year contract. The calculation of the cost of changes in other years would follow a similar pattern.

Assume that during the year immediately prior to the expiration of a contract, a firm maintained a labor force of 1,000 employees, 200 of whom were skilled, 800 of whom were unskilled. The skilled employees worked 440,000 productive hours (of which 60,000 were compensated at overtime rates) and the unskilled employees worked 1,760,000 hours (of which 240,000 were compensated at overtime rates). Total productive hours numbered 2,200,000. Table 5.1 indicates the key features of the old contract.

The best estimates of the marketing department indicate that sales during the first year of the new contract will increase by 8 percent. The production department has determined that an increase in production of 8 percent could be met by an increase in the number of productive labor hours of approximately 5 percent. The increase in hours would be in the same ratio of skilled to unskilled hours as the firm had operated in under in the past. Since the firm used 2,200,000 productive hours in the previous year, it would now require an additional 110,000 hours, or a total of 2,310,000 hours.

TABLE 5.1

KEY FEATURES OF OLD CONTRACT

I. Direct Wages
   Skilled $7.00 per hour
   Unskilled   4.00 per hour

II. Overtime
   Time and one-half for hours in excess of 40.

III. Holidays
   10 paid holidays per year.

IV. Vacations
   0-5   years service   2 weeks
   5-10 years service   3 weeks
   10-20 years service   4 weeks
   over 20 years service 5 weeks
   During past year vacations averaged 12½ days per employee.

V. Miscellaneous Paid Leave
   Paid leave granted for death in family, illness, jury duty, and military
   service. During past year miscellaneous leave averaged 3 days per
   employee.

VI. Accident and Sickness Insurance and Pensions
   Comprehensive plans, paid for entirely by employer.

VII. Supplemental Unemployment Benefits
   Comprehensive plan under which employer contributions depend on
   level of funding. Employees are eligible for unemployment benefits
   for a period of up to 26 weeks.

The production department has been disturbed about the large percentage of hours compensated at overtime rates. It has determined that overall labor costs could be reduced by hiring additional employees. It has been decided, therefore, that during the first year of the new contract the firm shall hire 100 new employees. Each new worker can be expected to perform approximately 1,900 hours of productive service during the year—a total of 190,000 hours. Because only 110,000 additional hours would be required to increase production, the remaining 80,000 hours contributed by the new employees could be used to reduce the number of overtime hours.

Since both the size and the rate mix of the labor force will change in the first year of the new contract, it is necessary, in order to compute the increase in labor costs attributable to changes in the contract independent of other planned operating changes, to first determine the cost of labor under the old contract assuming the new size and rate mix. Table 5.2 indicates such *pro forma* costs.

TABLE 5.2

PRO FORMA LABOR COSTS UNDER OLD CONTRACT ASSUMING NEW SIZE AND COMPOSITION OF LABOR FORCE AND NEW MIX OF STRAIGHT-TIME AND OVERTIME HOURS

Number of employees
    Skilled   220
    Unskilled   880

Number of productive hours
    Skilled   462,000 (including 44,000 overtime)
    Unskilled   1,848,000 (including 176,000 overtime)
                  2,310,000   220,000

I. Direct Wages
   Skilled
      462,000 hours x $7.00 per hour $3,234,000
      44,000 hours x $3.50 per overtime hour   154,000 $3,388,000
   Unskilled
      1,848,000 hours x $4.00 per hour $7,392,000
      176,000 hours x $2.00 per overtime hour   352,000   7,744,000 $11,132,000

II. Holidays
   Skilled
   220 men x 10 holidays x 8 hours x $7.00 $ 123,200
   Unskilled
   880 men x 10 holidays x 8 hours x $4.00   281,600   404,800

III. Vacations
   Skilled
   220 men x 12 days x 8 hours x $7.00 $ 147,840
   Unskilled
   880 men x 12 days x 8 hours x $4.00   337,920   485,760

IV. Miscellaneous Paid Leave
   Skilled
   220 men x 3 days x 8 hours x $7.00   36,960
   Unskilled
   880 men x 3 days x 8 hours x $7.00   147,840   184,800
           Total wage payments $12,207,360

TABLE 5.2—Contd.

V. *Accident and Sickness Insurance*	
1,100 men x $240 per year	264,000
VI. *Pension*	
Per actuary	500,000
VII. *Supplemental Unemployment Benefits*	
2,310,000 productive hours x $.05 per hour	115,500
VIII. *Payroll Taxes*	
Payroll taxes have previously averaged 6% of total wages;	
6% of 12,207,360 (new total wages)	732,442
Total cost	$13,819,302

The costs of some benefits such as holidays, miscellaneous paid leave and accident and sickness insurance, which are functions of the number of employees, are simply 10 percent (the increase in number of employees) greater than they actually were in the past year. Similarly, the cost of SUB, which is dependent upon the number of productive hours, is 5 percent (the increase in productive hours) greater than in the previous year. The *pro forma* cost of direct wages, however, has to be recomputed because the ratio of straight-time to overtime hours will change in the new contract period from what it was in the previous period. The cost of vacation pay has to be recalculated because the composition of the workforce in terms of length of service will change. Whereas in the previous year the number of vacation days averaged 12½ per employee, the addition of 100 new employees, each of whom will receive only 10 days of vacation, will lower the average to 12 days. In calculating the *pro forma* total of payroll taxes it is assumed that the ratio of payroll taxes to total payroll applicable to the previous period will continue unchanged.

Table 5.3 summarizes the major changes in the new contract. The cost of the revisions must, of course, be calculated using the projected, rather than the historical number and rate mix of productive hours, and size and composition of the labor force.

TABLE 5.3

SUMMARY OF MAJOR CHANGES IN NEW CONTRACT

I. Direct wages
Increase base wage rates by 6%, i.e., from $7.00 to $7.42 for skilled workers and from $4.00 to $4.24 for unskilled workers.

II. Overtime
Pay employees double time instead of time and one-half for work on Saturdays.

III. Holidays
Increase the number of paid holidays from 10 to 11.

IV. Vacations
Increase the length of vacation for workers with over 10 years' service by 1 week.

V. Cost-of-Living Bonus
Grant $.01 per hour bonus for each 0.5-point increase in cost-of-living index. The cost-of-living bonus will be computed semi-annually and will not be incorporated into the base wage rate. The bonus will be paid only on productive labor hours.

VI. Supplemental Unemployment Benefits
Increase by 4 weeks length of time employees will be eligible for benefits. Increase maximum company contribution to SUB fund from $.05 to $.06.

VII. Accident and Sickness Insurance and Pensions
Make miscellaneous improvements in plans.

Direct Wages

The cost of the 6-percent increase in direct wages can be computed by multiplying the number of anticipated productive hours by the differences between the old and the new rates. Thus:

Skilled:	462,000 hours x $.42/hour	$194,040
Unskilled:	1,848,000 hours x $.24/hour	443,520
		$637,560

The secondary effects of the wage increase (the impact of the increase on fringe benefits and payroll taxes) will be computed, after the cost of the changes in benefits has been determined.

Overtime

The proposed contract requires that work on Saturday be compensated at doubletime rather than time and one-half. The production department has estimated that 15 percent of all overtime has been in the past, and will be in the future, performed on Saturday. Fifteen percent of *planned* overtime hours represents 6,600 skilled hours and 26,400 unskilled hours. The additional cost, based on the old rates (the impact of the wage increase will be accounted for in the fringe "roll-up" percentage), is one half the base rates, or $3.50 and $2.00 per skilled and unskilled hour, respectively. The firm will, however, also incur payroll taxes on the additional wages. In the past payroll taxes have averaged 6 percent of compensation paid. But the same percentage is not necessarily appropriate for determining the taxes on the incremental wages. Payroll taxes apply only on earnings up to a maximum level. For example, Social Security taxes in 1972 were assessed on only the first $9,000 of earnings. To the extent that an employee has earned over the maximum, payroll taxes would have to be paid on the additional wages attributable to the increase in overtime pay. The accounting department of the firm has estimated that the earnings composition of the employee population is such that, *on average,* the tax rate applicable to incremental earnings is 3 percent. That is, any increase in corporate wages will result in a 3-percent increase in payroll taxes.

The cost of the contract change pertaining to overtime is, therefore:

Skilled:	6,600 hours x $3.50/hour	$23,100
Unskilled:	26,400 hours x $2.00/hour	52,800
		75,900
	Payroll taxes @ 3%	2,277
	Total cost	$78,177

Holidays

The firm estimates that, although eight productive hours per man will be lost because of the increase in the number of holidays from 10 to 11, 50 percent of the production scheduled for the extra holiday could be recovered in the course of normal working hours on other days. The remaining 50 percent would have to be rescheduled during overtime hours. Thus, the cost of the additional holiday is 50 percent of the hours lost times the appropriate overtime rates, plus payroll taxes (at the 3-percent incremental rate) on the extra overtime wages:

Skilled: 220 men x 8 holiday hours x
                  $10.50 per hour x 50% $ 9,240
Unskilled: 880 men x 8 holiday hours x
                  $6.00 per hour x 50%   21,120
                                                          $30,360
                        Payroll taxes @ 3%   911
                                    Total cost $31,271

Vacations

By reviewing personnel files the firm has determined that 200 employees, 50 skilled and 150 unskilled, have been with the company for over 10 years and are thereby eligible for an additional five days of vacation. The firm will therefore lose the services of skilled employees for 2,000 productive hours (50 employees times 40 hours) and of unskilled employees for 6,000 hours (150 employees times 40 hours). The production department has determined that the lost production attributable to the skilled workers could most effectively be recovered during overtime hours, but that the lost production of unskilled workers could best be recouped by hiring temporary employees for the summer months. The production department has estimated that 20 percent of the lost time of the skilled workers and 36 percent of the lost time of the unskilled employees could be made up during regular working hours. Thus, only 1,600 hours of skilled labor (80 percent of the 2,000 hours lost) would have to be compensated at overtime rates. To substitute for the unskilled employees, 12 unskilled workers would have to be hired for an eight-week period. The new employees, who would be paid at regular straight-time rates, would work a total of 3,840 hours (12 employees times eight weeks times 40 hours per week) and would thereby recover the required 64 percent of the 6,000 unskilled hours lost. The personnel department has estimated that the cost of hiring and training the temporary employees would be $500, and the cost of providing miscellaneous benefits for which they are eligible and of which they are likely to take advantage would be $150. Cost of the revisions pertaining to vacations would, therefore, be:

Skilled: 1,600 hours x $10.50
                  (overtime rate) $16,800

```
Unskilled: 3,840 hours x $  4.00
           (straight-time rate)                        15,360
                                                       $32,160
                Payroll taxes @ 3%                        965
                                                       $33,125

Cost of hiring and training new
   temporary employees              $500
Cost of providing additional
   benefits                          150
Additional payroll taxes and
   miscellaneous costs               100           750
           Total cost                            $33,875
```

As before, payroll taxes are computed using the marginal rate of 3 percent. The payroll taxes on the earnings of the temporary employees, however, are likely to be considerably greater than 3 percent since, if they are employed for only eight weeks, their entire wages will be subject to tax. An estimate of the payroll taxes in addition to those computed using the 3-percent rate is included in the final item, "Additional payroll taxes and miscellaneous costs."

Cost-of-Living Bonus

The new contract provides that, for the first time, earnings of employees will depend, in part, upon the cost of living. For each 0.5-point increase in the Department of Labor's Consumer Price Index, workers will receive a bonus of $.01 per hour. Adjustments in the size of the bonus will be made semi-annually, but the bonus will be incorporated into the base wage rate only at year end. Until the bonus is built into the wage rate it will be paid only on productive hours—it will have no effect on compensated time off or overtime premium.

After reviewing economic forecasts and consulting with outside economists, the firm has estimated that the Consumer Price Index will increase by 2.0 points during the first six months of the contract. Hence, employees will be entitled to a $.04 per hour bonus in the last six months of the year. The firm assumes that the 2,310,-000 productive hours that it has scheduled for the first year of the new contract will be spread evenly throughout the year, so that the bonus will have to be paid on one half the productive hours, or 1,155,000 hours. The cost of the bonus is, therefore:

1,155,000 hours x $.04	$46,200
Payroll taxes @ 3%	1,386
Total cost	$47,586

Supplemental Unemployment Benefits

Under the new agreement, employees will be eligible to receive unemployment benefits, in the event that they are laid off, for up to 30 weeks instead of the previous 26. To make certain that sufficient resources are available to fulfill the new obligations, management and the union have agreed that the schedule of required company contributions to the SUB fund should be revised. The company has estimated that, as a result of the changes, its cents-per-productive-hour contribution will increase during the first year of the contract from $.05 to $.06. The cost of the change would be:

2,310,000 hours x $.01	$23,100

Accident and Sickness Insurance; Pensions

The company has agreed to make substantial improvements in both its accident and sickness insurance programs and its pension plan. The insurance company that writes the accident and sickness policy has estimated that the additional costs attributable to the improvements will be $100 per man. Consulting actuaries have determined that the modifications in the pension plan will require that the company increase its annual contribution to the pension fund by $150,000. Costs of the improvements would be:

Accident and	1100 employees x	
sickness insurance	$100 per man	$110,000
Pension		150,000
		$260,000

Effect of Direct Wage Increases on Fringe Benefits

The 6-percent increase in wage rates will result both in higher payroll taxes and in a greater cost of providing fringe benefits which are a function of the base wage rate (e.g., overtime premiums, holidays, vacations and miscellaneous paid time off). The dollar effect of the wage increase on payroll taxes and benefits can be determined by computing both a "roll-up" percentage and a "package roll-up percentage" and multiplying the sum of the two percentages by the dollar amount of the direct wage increase. The "roll-up" percentage represents the ratio of the cost of the old benefits to direct wages paid (both cost of old benefits and direct wages paid being determined on the basis of provisions in the old contract about to expire). The percentage must be calculated using not the actual amounts paid, but instead the amounts that would have been paid given the projected, rather than the historical, size and composition of the work force (the amounts indicated in Table 5.2).

Cost of benefits and taxes based on old wage rate:

Overtime premium

Skilled	$154,000		
Unskilled	352,000	$ 506,000	
Holidays		404,800	
Vacations		485,760	
Miscellaneous paid leave		184,800	
Payroll taxes		366,220	$ 1,947,580

÷

Direct wages:

Skilled	$3,234,000	
Unskilled	7,392,000	10,626,000
Roll-up percentage		18.33%

Estimated payroll taxes based on old wage rates are, from Table 5.2, 6 percent of total payroll of $12,207,360 or $732,442. The payroll taxes indicated above represent but 3 percent of the $12,207,360. The lower percentage, which represents the marginal tax rate, must be used because the change in wages will not increase payroll taxes by the full 6 percent, since, as noted earlier, the earnings of some employees are already above the maximum amount subject to tax. Were the higher rather than the lower amount used, the roll-up percentage would overstate the future effect of wage increases on fringe benefits and payroll taxes.

The "package roll-up" percentage is determined by dividing the cost (based on the old wage rates) of the new benefits which are affected by a change in wage rates by the *old* direct-wage costs.

Cost of new benefits based on old wage rate (per previous computations):

Saturday overtime	$ 78,177	
Vacations	33,125	
Holidays	31,271	$ 142,573
		÷
Direct wages:		
Skilled	$3,234,000	
Unskilled	7,392,000	$10,626,000
Package roll-up percentage		1.34%

The cost of the additional vacation benefit, it should be noted, excludes the $750 which represents expenses of hiring and training new employees since it is assumed that such amounts will not be affected by the change in the direct wage rate.

The total roll-up percentage is 18.33 percent plus 1.34 percent, or 19.67 percent. The cost of the direct wage increase has been computed to be $637,560, so the secondary effect of the wage increase on benefits and payroll taxes would be:

Direct wage increase	$637,560
Total roll-up %	x 19.67%
Impact of direct wage increase on fringe benefits and payroll taxes	$125,408

"Spillover"

The firm currently employs, and expects to continue to employ, 50 white-collar workers who are not covered by the union agreement. Total employment costs attributable to such workers in the past year were $500,000. The firm expects that, as a result of the new contract, exempt employees too will receive a 6-percent wage increase and their fringe benefit package will also be improved. Following procedures identical to those used to compute the cost of the changes in the wages and benefits of the covered employees, the firm has calculated that the cost of increases in the compensation of the exempt employees will be $45,000.

Prices

The company is in a highly competitive industry, and the firm's sales manager believes that the present market for the firm's products is sufficiently soft that the company will be unable to pass on to consumers even a small portion of the additional labor costs. But the firm does a substantial portion of its business with the government under cost-plus-fixed-fee agreements, and it estimates that the government will absorb $475,000 of the increased labor costs.

Summary of Costs

The cost of the contract changes is summarized in Table 5.4. Net cost of the revisions is $806,977 after taking into account the probable effects of both the compensation of exempt employees and the additional revenue to be generated from the government contracts. When divided by the anticipated number of productive hours, 2,310,000, the increase is $.3493 per hour. The cents-per-hour term, however, must be used with caution; it bears little resemblance to the "traditional" cents-per-hour expression. It indicates not the average increase in compensation, but rather the net cost, after considering the additional costs and revenues attributable to the contract revisions. For bargaining purposes the more relevant cents-per-hour figure is likely to be the cost of the increase ascribable only to the compensation of the employees covered by the contract—$12,236,977 or $.5344 per hour. To the extent that a percentage expression is desired, the dollar cost of the increase must include only those elements of compensation that are included in the original cost. Since computation of the original cost excludes consideration of revenues, so also must computation of the increase. Total compensation cost (including that of "exempt" employees) under the old agreement (based on projected size and mix of workforce) would have been $14,319,302; cost of the increase (excluding change in revenue) is $1,281,977. Therefore, the percentage increase in compensation is $1,281,977 divided by $14,319,302, or 8.95 percent.

TABLE 5.4

COST OF OLD CONTRACT AND COST OF REVISIONS—TOTAL
COST AND CENTS-PER-PRODUCTIVE-HOUR COST
(Assuming new size and composition of labor force and mix of
straight-time and overtime hours. Based on 2,310,000 productive hours)

	Old Contract		Revisions	
	Total	Cents per Hour	Total	Cents per Hour
Direct Wages	$10,626,000	$4.6000	$ 637,560	$.2760
Overtime Premium	506,000	.2190	78,177	.0338
Holidays	404,800	.1752	31,271	.0135
Vacations	485,760	.2103	33,875	.0147
Miscellaneous Paid Leave	184,800	.0800	—	—
Accident and Sickness Insurance	264,000	.1143	110,000	.0476
Supplementary Unemployment Benefits	115,500	.0500	23,100	.0100
Cost-of-Living Adjustment	—	—	47,586	.0206
Pension	500,000	.2165	150,000	.0649
Payroll Taxes	732,442	.3171	—(a)	—(a)
Effect of Direct Wage Increase on Fringe Benefits	—	—	125,408	.0543
Total "Direct" Cost of Contract Revisions	$13,819,302	$5.9824	$1,236,977	$.5354
Add: Compensation of "Exempt" employees	500,000	.2165	45,000	.0195
Total Cost Including that Applicable to "Exempt" Employees	$14,319,302	$6.1989	1,281,977	.5549
Less Increase in Revenues Attributable to Cost-Plus Government Contracts	—	—	475,000	.2056
Net Cost of Contract Revision	$14,319,302	$6.1989	$ 806,977	$.3493

(a) Increase in payroll taxes is included in "Effect of Direct Wage Increase
on Fringe Benefits."

BASIC ASSUMPTIONS OF MODEL

In determining the financial impact of a proposed contract,
the timing of wage increases is obviously critical. An increase

granted at the beginning of a contract is more costly than one which is spread over the entire contract. An increase of $1.00 per hour, for example, will cost the firm $3.00 ($1.00 + $1.00 + $1.00) over the life of a three-year contract. An increase of $1.00 spread evenly over the contract will cost the firm only $2.00. The annual wage increase will be $.33 per year, so the cumulative increases will be $.33, $.67, and $1.00. The total cost of the increase will, therefore, be $.33 + $.67 + $1.00 or $2.00. Ignoring all considerations other than direct cost, a firm would obviously prefer an increase of $1.00 spread evenly over the life of the contract to an increase of $1.00 that is "front-loaded," or granted at the beginning of the contract.

When the time value of money is taken into account, however, the problem of selecting among alternative patterns of increases becomes more complex. An increase granted in the second or third years of a contract can no longer be equated with an increase of an identical amount given in the first year of a contract. The "present value" of the increases in each of the three years can be obtained by applying the standard formula for present value:[6]

$$(6\text{-}1) \qquad\qquad PV = F(1+r)^{-n}$$

where

PV = Present value of a given sum
F = Equivalent future value n periods hence
r = Discount rate [7]

The present values of $1 at various rates of interest and over various periods of time are indicated in Table 5.5. If the firm has selected a discount rate of 20 percent, then an increase of $1.00 per hour

---

[6] It is assumed in this and subsequent formulas that interest is compounded annually and that all cash flows take place at the end of the year. Both assumptions are in accord with the conventions of the literature of capital budgeting, but both may be easily modified (if one wishes, for example, to assume that wages are paid weekly) by adjusting the equations. For a discussion of the required adjustments, see FINANCIAL COMPOUND INTEREST AND ANNUITY TABLES, C. H. Gushee, ed. (Boston: Financial Publishing Co., 1970), Ch. XI.

[7] "The cost of capital" is the most popular answer to the question of what discount rate should be used in calculating the present value of future cash flows. For a discussion of several approaches to computing cost of capital, see Harold Bierman, Jr., and Seymour Smidt, THE CAPITAL BUDGETING DECISION, third edition (New York: Macmillan, 1971), Ch. 8-10.

granted at the beginning of the third year of a three-year contract is equivalent to an increase of $.83 granted at the beginning of the second year and $.69 granted at the beginning of the first year. The "present value" of each of the three increases is $.69.

TABLE 5.5

PRESENT VALUE OF $1

Years	6%	10%	14%	18%	20%
1	0.943	0.909	0.877	0.847	0.833
2	0.890	0.826	0.769	0.718	0.694
3	0.840	0.751	0.675	0.609	0.579
4	0.792	0.683	0.592	0.516	0.482
5	0.747	0.621	0.519	0.437	0.402
6	0.705	0.564	0.456	0.370	0.335
7	0.665	0.513	0.400	0.314	0.279
8	0.627	0.467	0.351	0.266	0.233
9	0.592	0.424	0.308	0.225	0.194
10	0.558	0.386	0.270	0.191	0.162
11	0.527	0.350	0.237	0.162	0.135
12	0.497	0.319	0.208	0.137	0.112
13	0.469	0.290	0.182	0.116	0.093
14	0.442	0.263	0.160	0.099	0.078
15	0.417	0.239	0.140	0.084	0.065

Suppose that a firm is currently paying its employees at the rate of $1.00 per hour and is in the process of negotiating a new *two-year* contract. Management has proposed a front-loaded increase of $.20 per hour. The present value of such a proposal may be computed by discounting back to the present the wages in each of the two years of the contract. Assume that the firm's cost of capital is 20 percent. Thus (employing the present values in the "20%" column of Table 5.5):

$$\text{Year 1} \quad \$1.20 \times .833 = \$ .9996$$
$$\text{Year 2} \quad \$1.20 \times .694 = \$ .8328$$
$$\text{Total present value} \quad \underline{\$1.8324}$$

The present value of the proposal is $1.8324. The union, however, has demanded a total increase of more than $.20, but it is willing to accept the increase spread evenly over the two years of the

contract. What increase spread over the two years could management offer and still be as well off as if the union had accepted its
original proposal?

If X denotes the increase during the first year of the contract,
then $1.00 + X represents the wage during the first year and
$1.00 + 2X represents the wage during the second year. The pres-
ent value of the contract is, therefore, the sum of the present values
of the wages during each of the years of the contract, which must
equal $1.8324, the present value of the front-loaded contract.
Hence (again using present values from Table 5.5):

$$(1.00 + X) \ .833 + (1.00 + 2X) \ .694 = 1.8324$$

X, therefore, equals .1375. Thus, management could offer the union
increases of $.1375 in both the first and second years and the wages
in the two years would be, respectively, $1.1375 and $1.2750. The
present value of the contract would be the same $1.8324:

Year 1	$1.1375 x .833 =	$ .9475
Year 2	$1.2750 x .694 =	$ .8849
	Total present value	$1.8324

A question arises, however. Would management really be indifferent as between a front-loaded increase of $.20 per hour and a
"spread" increase of $.275 even if each does have the same present
value? Near the expiration of the contract, when the two parties
return to the bargaining table, the existing wage under the spread
contract would be $1.275 but only $1.20 under the front-loaded
contract. Since the wage in effect is likely to be the foundation upon
which new increases are negotiated, management would appear to
be in a superior position had the settlement been based upon the
front-loaded increase, which results in a lower wage at the expiration of the contract. Contracts negotiated in the present and future
are obviously not independent of those which have been signed in
the past, and since wages, especially in unionized industries, tend to
be characterized by a "ratchet effect" (they often increase, but seldom decrease), any wage increase negotiated in the present will in
all probability be built into the wage structure permanently. Unlike
many capital projects which have determinate, albeit sometimes
difficult to estimate, useful lives, the effects of wage contracts may
continue to be felt over an indefinite number of years.

Two alternatives to analyzing a wage increase over only the life of the contract itself are to evaluate it either as a perpetuity or over a time period specified by the decision-maker himself. If the contract were treated as a perpetuity, it would be necessary to compute the present value of the increase as though it were an annuity over an infinite number of years. The perpetuity approach was discussed with several of the industrial relations managers and finance officers interviewed. While they recognize that it is reasonable to evaluate a contract change over a period longer than that of the agreement itself, they indicated that because of the difficulties of making long-range projections, they would be unwilling to give weight to possible effects of decisions made in the present on contracts to be signed in the very distant future.

The other alternative—that of evaluating the contract over a time period specified by the decision-maker—was unanimously favored by the managers to whom it was described. The decision-maker would be able to state explicitly the number of years (or contracts) over which he wished to consider the financial effects of a proposal. Most managers interviewed indicated that the time span which they would consider relevant would be short, generally five to 10 years. In this chapter the optional-time-perspective alternative will be employed in developing the model so that the manager can evaluate a contract over the number of years of his choice.

Before the cost of a wage increase can be evaluated over several contract periods, additional assumptions regarding the behavior of wages in future years must be made. At what rate will wages increase each contract after the first? What pattern (e.g., front-loaded or spread) will increases follow in future contracts? What effect will the wage rate at the expiration of the initial contract have on wage rates of future contracts?

The present value of a contract depends upon the rate at which wages will increase in the future. The anticipated rate of increase, however, is unlikely to be the same for firms in all industries or even for one firm at different points in time. Provision must be made in the discounted cash flow model, therefore, to permit the decision-maker to specify his own estimate of the per-contract percentage by which wages will increase.

Although labor and management may reach agreement on a particular pattern of increases, they are by no means committed to that same pattern when negotiating future contracts. In some industries, of course, the pattern is fixed by tradition, but the two parties nevertheless have the option, at each series of bargaining sessions, to consider alternative patterns. Comparisons among alternate proposals can be greatly simplified if as many variables as are feasible are held constant for all proposals under consideration. Thus, contract evaluation may be facilitated by assuming that all wage agreements in the future will follow an identical pattern. In developing the model it will be assumed, therefore, that contracts subsequent to the first will be front-loaded.[8]

The wage rate at the expiration of the first contract depends upon the firm's choice of pattern of increases. Presumably, if an increase is spread over the length of the contract, the ending wage rate would be higher than if it were front-loaded. If wages are assumed to increase by a fixed percentage each contract after the first, then over the years there would be an ever-widening gap between the resulting wages if the first contract were front-loaded and those if it were spread. For example, if the initial wage were $1.00 and wages increase at the rate of 20 percent in each two-year contract, then wages over the next several contracts if the first contract were front-loaded would be:

Year	Wage	Year	Wage
1	$1.200	5	$1.728
2	1.200	6	1.728
3	1.440	7	2.074
4	1.440	8	2.074

If, however, the increase in the first contract were spread over the two years then the wages would be:

Year	Wage	Year	Wage
1	$1.137	5	$1.836
2	1.275	6	1.836
3	1.530	7	2.203
4	1.530	8	2.203

Whereas wages would be only $.075 apart after the second year, they would be $.129 apart after the eighth.

---

[8] An alternative assumption that contracts subsequent to the first follow the same pattern as the first has also been tested. The differences in present values attributable to choice of assumption were found to be relatively small.

In practice, such a divergence is unlikely. Wages, over a period of years, are determined by many factors: the supply of and demand for workers with particular skills; the growth of the economy; the bargaining strengths of the respective parties. As the number of years increases, the wage rate at the expiration of the initial contract can be expected to exert a decreasing influence on future wage rates. To avoid the divergence, the present-value model will incorporate the assumption that wages will increase by a fixed percentage each contract, but only by a fixed percentage of wages based on a hypothetical front-loaded contract. The assumed contract will provide for an initial wage increment equal in percentage to that by which the manager anticipates that wages will rise in subsequent contracts.

The wages over the next four contracts if the first contract were front-loaded, and the anticipated rate by which wages will increase over the next several contracts is 20 percent, would be the same as those indicated previously:

Year	Wage	Year	Wage
1	$1.20	5	$1.728
2	1.20	6	1.728
3	1.44	7	2.074
4	1.44	8	2.074

But if the contract were spread, only the wages over the first two years would remain unchanged at $1.1375 and $1.2750. The increase in the second contract would not be 20 percent of $1.275. Instead it would be 20 percent of $1.20 (the front-loaded wage), plus an additional $.075. The total increase, therefore, would be $.24 plus $.075 or $.315, and the new wage would be $1.515. The additional $.075 represents the difference between the initial wage under an assumed front-loaded increase of 20 percent and that under the spread increase. The difference can be viewed as a "premium," which will be built into the wage structure and remain constant throughout the period under consideration. The increase at the beginning of the third contract would be 20 percent of $1.44 (the wage at the beginning of the third contract under the assumed front-loaded contract) plus the premium of $.075. The increase, therefore, would be $.288 plus $.075 or $.363, and the new wage would be $1.728. At the beginning of the fourth contract the wage would be $2.149, again $.075 greater than it would be under the front-loaded contract. Thus, the wages over the eight-year period would be:

Year	Wage	Year	Wage
1	$1.1375	5	$1.8030
2	1.2750	6	1.8030
3	1.5150	7	2.1490
4	1.5150	8	2.1490

In summary, some key features of the present-value model as adjusted to evaluate labor contracts are:

1. The number of contracts over which proposed wage increases are to be assessed must be specified. So too must an appropriate discount rate (presumably an internal rate of return or rate of cost of capital) and an estimate of the rate by which wages will increase each contract after the first.

2. All contracts after the first will be front-loaded.

3. Wages will increase by a fixed percentage of the wages of a hypothetical front-loaded contract. The wage increase during the first contract after the hypothetical front-loaded contract will be determined by multiplying the wage rate under the expiring contract by the percentage by which the decision-maker expects wages to increase each contract after the first. The difference between the actual wage proposed and the wage under the hypothetical front-loaded contract will be a "premium" that will be built into the wage structure and remain constant for all contracts following the first.

Returning to the question of whether management would be indifferent as between a front-loaded increase of $1.20 per hour and a spread increase of $1.275 when the two have identical present values over the two-year contract period, it becomes clear that management would prefer the front-loaded contract if its perspective were longer than just one contract period. Evaluated over four contract periods (eight years) the present value of the front-loaded contract would be $5.70:

Year	Wage	Present Value of $1	Present Value of Wage
1	$1.200	$.8333	$1.0000
2	1.200	.6944	.8333

3	1.440	.5787	.8333
4	1.440	.4823	.6945
5	1.728	.4019	.6945
6	1.728	.3349	.5787
7	2.074	.2791	.5787
8	2.074	.2326	.4824
			$5.6954

The present value of the spread contract, however, would be $5.87:

Year	Wage	Present Value of $1	Present Value of Wage
1	$1.1375	$.8333	$ .9478
2	1.2750	.6944	.8854
3	1.5150	.5787	.8767
4	1.5150	.4823	.7307
5	1.8030	.4019	.7246
6	1.8030	.3349	.6038
7	2.1490	.2791	.5998
8	2.1490	.2326	.4999
			$5.8687

Since the front-loaded increase is the less costly of the two, company negotiators would attempt to reach a settlement based on it, rather than on the spread increase.

APPLICATION OF THE MODEL

The specific equations which constitute the model are derived and explained in Appendix II.

The utility of the model is that it enables management to formulate a wage offer that it believes it can afford and then determine other patterns of increases that will have the same cost. Although the union may be adverse to the original offer, it may be willing to accept the alternatives.

Suppose that management has decided that it can afford increases of $.15 in the first year of a three-year contract, $.10 in the second year and $.05 in the third year. The current wage is $1, the time perspective of management is four contract periods, the appropriate discount rate is 18 percent, and management anticipates that over the next several years wage rates will rise at a per-contract rate of 20 percent. By discounting the wages in each year of the contract back to the present (or by employing equation 6-7 in Appendix II), the present value of the offer can be computed to be $7.24.

Year	Wage	Present Value of $1	Present Value of Wage
1	$1.15	$.8475	$ .9746
2	1.25	.7182	.8977
3	1.30	.6086	.7912
4	1.54	.5158	.7943
5	1.54	.4371	.6731
6	1.54	.3704	.5704
7	1.83	.3139	.5744
8	1.83	.2660	.4867
9	1.83	.2255	.4126
10	2.17	.1911	.4147
11	2.17	.1619	.3513
12	2.17	.1372	.2977
			$7.2387

The wages for the 12-year period are based on the assumptions indicated previously.

Management can now use the equations of the model to develop alternative offers that will have the same present value of $7.24. By setting the equation for a front-loaded contract (equation 6-3a) equal to $7.24, management could determine that an immediate increase of $.266 (and no increase during the next two years) would have the same cost as its initial offer. Wages, based on the previously described assumptions, and their present worth over the period of 12 years would be:

Year	Wage	Present Value of $1	Present Value of Wage
1	$1.266	$.8475	$1.0729
2	1.266	.7182	.9092
3	1.266	.6086	.7705

4	1.506	.5158	.7768
5	1.506	.4371	.6583
6	1.506	.3704	.5579
7	1.794	.3139	.5631
8	1.794	.2660	.4772
9	1.794	.2255	.4045
10	2.140	.1911	.4090
11	2.140	.1619	.3465
12	2.140	.1372	.2936
			$7.2395

By setting the equation for a spread contract (Equation 6-6) equal to $7.24, management could ascertain another pattern of increases which it could propose to its union and be no worse off than if it had accepted the first. The appropriate spread contract offer would require increases of $.107 during each of the three years:

Year	Wage	Present Value of $1	Present Value of Wage
1	$1.107	$.8475	$ .9382
2	1.214	.7182	.8719
3	1.320	.6086	.8034
4	1.560	.5158	.8046
5	1.560	.4371	.6819
6	1.560	.3704	.5778
7	1.848	.3139	.5801
8	1.848	.2660	.4916
9	1.848	.2255	.4167
10	2.194	.1911	.4193
11	2.194	.1619	.3552
12	2.194	.1372	.3010
			$7.2417

The slight discrepancies among the three total present values are attributable to rounding of the wage rates and the present values. The model serves to indicate two additional wage packages that management could propose and be equally as well off as if the union had accepted the original offer. Each has a present value of $7.24:

Year of Contract	Original Proposal	Front-loaded Contract	Spread Contract
1	$1.15	$1.266	$1.107
2	1.25	1.266	1.214
3	1.30	1.266	1.320

The model would be especially valuable if it were incorporated into a computer software package, particularly one which would enable an executive to enter into the computer, via a conveniently located terminal, proposals which he is considering. The computer would return to him alternative proposals which would have the same present value. The program would allow him to test, with minimum cost and effort, numerous wage combinations. Exhibit I contains the printout from such a program.

EXHIBIT I

PRINTOUT FROM A COMPUTER PROGRAM DESIGNED TO IDENTIFY EQUALLY ACCEPTABLE WAGE PROPOSALS
(Information entered into terminal by executive is indicated in italics)

$RUN
#EXECUTION BEGINS

WHAT IS THE INTERNAL RATE OF RETURN OF YOUR COMPANY? WRITE IN DECIMAL FORM, I.E. .05
.16

BY WHAT PERCENT DO YOU EXPECT WAGES TO INCREASE EACH CONTRACT AFTER THE FIRST? WRITE IN DECIMAL FORM, I.E. .20
.18

WHAT IS THE LENGTH, IN YEARS, OF YOUR CONTRACT?
3

WHAT IS YOUR TIME PERSPECTIVE, IN NUMBER OF CONTRACTS?
3

WHAT IS THE PRESENT WAGE?
5.00

INDICATE, IN DOLLARS, THE PROPOSED INCREASES DURING THE FIRST CONTRACT. TYPE THE INCREASE FOR EACH YEAR ON A NEW LINE.
.50
.35
.15

EXHIBIT I—Contd.

RATE = .16
GROWTH RATE = .18
CONTRACT LENGTH = 3
PERSPECTIVE = 3
CURRENT WAGE = 5.00

PROPOSED INCREASES = 0.50   0.35   0.15

IS ABOVE DATA CORRECT? ANSWER YES OR NO
YES

YOU PROPOSED A TOTAL INCREASE OF 20.0 PERCENT
ALTERNATIVELY YOU WOULD BE AS WELL OFF BY GIVING
THE FOLLOWING INCREASE SPREAD OVER THE LIFE OF
THE CONTRACT:
PERCENT INCREASE: 21.48
TOTAL DOLLAR INCREASE: 1.074
ANNUAL DOLLAR INCREASE: 0.358
NEW WAGE AT END OF CONTRACT: 6.074

OR YOU COULD ALSO HAVE PROPOSED A FRONT-LOADED
CONTRACT AS FOLLOWS:
PERCENT INCREASE: 17.64
TOTAL DOLLAR INCREASE: 0.882
NEW WAGE AT END OF CONTRACT: 5.882

PRESENT VALUES OF PROPOSALS

CONTRACT NO.	YOUR PROPOSAL	EVEN SPREAD	FRONT LOADED
1	12.9328	12.7582	13.2108
2	23.0939	23.0257	23.2025
3	30.7589	30.7589	30.7589
4	36.5428	36.5865	36.4732
5	40.9085	40.9801	40.7944

DO YOU WANT TO TRY AGAIN? WRITE YES OR NO
NO

STOP
#EXECUTION TERMINATED
#$SIGNOFF

TABLES INDICATING ALTERNATIVE CONTRACT PROPOSALS

On the basis of the present-value formulas, a series of tables can be developed to enable management to evaluate and compare alternative contract proposals. Table 5.6 indicates the present values (per $1 per hour of wages) for various rates of discount, assuming that wages will increase by 20 percent each two-year contract after the first. Shown in the body of the table are the present values after each of several contracts. The present value, for example, of

TABLE 5.6

PRESENT VALUES OF *FRONT-LOADED* CONTRACTS AT
VARIOUS DISCOUNT RATES

(2-year Contracts; 20 Percent Per Contract Increases
in Wages; $1 Initial Wage)

Contract Number	Discount Rate					
	.04	.08	.12	.16	.20	.24
1	2.2633	2.1399	2.0281	1.9263	1.8333	1.7482
2	4.7743	4.3414	3.9682	3.6441	3.3611	3.1125
3	7.5602	6.6064	5.8241	5.1761	4.6342	4.1773
4	10.6511	8.9366	7.5996	6.5423	5.6952	5.0083
5	14.0804	11.3340	9.2981	7.7607	6.5793	5.6568
6	17.8850	13.8004	10.9229	8.8472	7.3161	6.1630
7	22.1061	16.3378	12.4773	9.8162	7.9301	6.5580
8	26.7892	18.9483	13.9642	10.6803	8.4417	6.8663
9	31.9851	21.6341	15.3867	11.4509	8.8681	7.1069
10	37.7497	24.3972	16.7475	12.1381	9.2234	7.2946

a contract providing for an initial wage of $1.20 after four contract periods, if the discount rate is 20 percent, is $5.6952. Table 5.7 shows the present values of a contract in which the initial increases are spread evenly over the first contract. The table assumes that wages will increase by 20 percent in each contract after the first and that the appropriate discount rate is 20 percent. The table shows the present values of contracts in which alternative amounts of premiums are paid. A premium of $.00 indicates that the wage after the first contract is $1.20—the same as it would be if the contract were front-loaded. Since the $.20 increase is spread over two years, however, the wage after the first year is $1.10 and that after the second is $1.20. A premium of $.02 indicates that the wage after the first contract is $1.22, or $.02 more than if the contract were front-loaded. Hence, the wage after the first year is $1.11, and that after the second is $1.22. Similarly, a premium of $.04 indicates that the wage after the first contract is $1.24; that of $.06 indicates a wage of $1.26. The present value, after four contracts, of a spread contract providing for a total increase of $1.22 can be determined from the table to be $5.6803.

Such tables might be useful to a manager in that they would enable him to find an equally acceptable alternative to a front-

TABLE 5.7

PRESENT VALUES OF *SPREAD* CONTRACTS AT
VARIOUS PREMIUMS [1]

(2-Year Contracts; 20-Percent-Per-Contract Increases
in Wages; 20-Percent Discount Rate; $1 Initial Wage)

Contract Number	Premium—Cents Per Hour					
	.00	.02	.04	.06	.08	.10
1	1.7500	1.7722	1.7944	1.8167	1.8389	1.8611
2	3.2778	3.3212	3.3647	3.4081	3.4515	3.4950
3	4.5509	4.6091	4.6673	4.7254	4.7836	4.8418
4	5.6119	5.6803	5.7487	5.8171	5.8855	5.9539
5	6.4960	6.5715	6.6470	6.7226	6.7981	6.8736
6	7.2328	7.3132	7.3937	7.4741	7.5546	7.6350
7	7.8468	7.9306	8.0145	8.0984	8.1823	8.2661
8	8.3584	8.4447	8.5309	8.6172	8.7034	8.7897
9	8.7848	8.8727	8.9606	9.0485	9.1364	9.2243
10	9.1401	9.2292	9.3182	9.4073	9.4963	9.5854

[1] All contracts after the first are assumed to be front-loaded.

loaded (or a spread) contract. Having found from Table 5.6, for example, that the present value of a proposal providing for a 20-percent increase that is front-loaded is $5.6952 after four contracts, he can scan the line applicable to a four-contract perspective in Table 5.7 to find the present value most closely approaching $5.6952. In this example, $5.6803 is closest to $5.6952, so a firm could pay a premium of slightly more than $.02, or an ending wage of slightly over $1.22 and be as well off as it would be if it were able to settle on a front-loaded increase of $.20. Tables for other discount rates, estimated growth rates and contract lengths can easily be formulated with the aid of a computer.

For convenience, the tables assume that the initial wage rate is $1. If the initial wage rate is something other than $1—as in practice it inevitably will be—all amounts in the table (present values and premiums) must be multiplied by the ratio of the initial wage to $1. Thus, the present value (over four contract periods) of an agreement providing for a 20-percent or $1 wage increase in a $5 initial wage would be $5.6952 times $5/$1 or $28.4760, and the premium that management could afford to pay if it granted a spread contract would be approximately 2 percent of $5, or $.10.

A GRAPHIC APPROACH TO ALTERNATIVE
CONTRACT PROPOSALS

Alternative contract proposals to which management would be indifferent may be represented graphically as well as algebraically. In Chart 1, the horizontal axis depicts the potential wage to be paid during the first year of a two-year contract. The vertical axis depicts the potential wage to be paid during the second year. Thus, point A indicates the wages to be paid under the front-loaded contract used in previous examples: $1.20 the first year; $1.20 the second year. Point B represents the wages to be paid under the spread contract: $1.112 the first year; $1.224 the second year. Line AB is an "indifference curve"; each point along the line represents a combination of wages requiring the same financial sacrifice. A contract prescribing wage rates of (approximately) $1.15 the first year and $1.213 the second (Point C) would be as acceptable to management as would the spread contract (Point B) or the front-loaded contract (Point A).

Similarly, management would "theoretically" be willing to pay wages represented by Points D and E. Point D denotes a wage of $1.25 the first year and $1.186 the second year. Only in rare circumstances, however, would a contract prescribing such a declining wage rate fall within management's set of realistic alternatives. Point E, on the other hand, represents a wage of $1.05 the first year and $1.24 the second. A contract providing for such a pattern of wage increases is "back-loaded"—the increase in the second year is greater than that in the first. Several managers interviewed expressed doubt that the unions which with they negotiate would be willing to accept a back-loaded contract. Points A and B, therefore, are the effective outside limits on the alternatives of management. To the right of Point A, the wage rate declines from one year to the next; to the left of Point B, the increases increase. If a contract were for three rather than two years, an indifference plane would have to be plotted on a "three-dimensional" graph.

The slope of the indifference curve gives an indication of the size of the premium that the firm can pay on a spread contract and still be as well off as if it had agreed to a front-loaded contract. If the curve is relatively flat, the premium is relatively small; the wages in the second years of both the front-loaded and the spread

CHART 1

Management "Indifference Line"

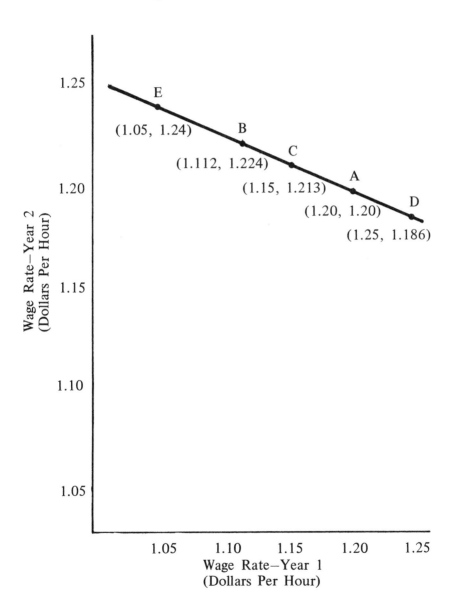

contracts are relatively close to one another. If the curve is steep, there is a great difference between the ending wages, and the premium is large.

REACTIONS OF MANAGERS TO THE
PRESENT-VALUE APPROACH

None of the firms at which interviews were conducted currently takes into account the time value of money in evaluating alternative contract proposals. No company, in fact, has even seriously considered introducing present values into its analyses.

The responses of executives interviewed toward the present-value approach ranged from skepticism to mild enthusiasm. Managers of firms, such as the one which uses the estimated planning volume, that perform comprehensive analyses of contract proposals were more receptive to the present-value approach than were those of firms that perform only superficial analyses. Several managers think that the present-value approach is a "good idea," or that "it appears as if it would be useful." The primary reservation expressed by the managers interviewed was that the additional information provided by the discounted cash flow model would have little influence upon the bargaining process. Some, for example, maintained that the unions with which they deal almost always want a front-loaded contract. Others said that in their industries' settlements usually follow a spread pattern. A few managers were fearful that the executives to whom they report would have difficulty interpreting contract costs expressed in terms of discounted dollars. None, however, thought that he himself would have such difficulty.

One manager, who was among the most optimistic about the potential of the present-value approach, pointed out that if management were to discount anticipated wage increases, it would also have to recognize, and discount, anticipated price increases. If a labor contract is front-loaded, price increases might also be front-loaded. His point is well taken. As previously emphasized, it is essential that management attempt to identify changes in all cash flows that are likely to be associated with changes in wages. It has been assumed throughout this section that the cents-per-hour proposals represent the *net* cents-per-hour outflow. Alternatively, management could ignore cents-per-hour amounts and instead compute the present value of the net *dollar* cash flows.

CHAPTER VI

A Brief Summary

DEFICIENCIES IN PRESENTLY USED PROCEDURES

The theme of this book is that despite their magnitude—for most firms they represent the single largest expenditure—labor costs are ineffectively controlled at the bargaining table. Presently used procedures to evaluate contract changes do not provide labor relations managers with an adequate understanding of the potential impact on profits of alternative proposals under consideration. Contract changes are often reviewed in the isolation of a labor relations department and, perhaps as a result, improper data are improperly analyzed.

With few exceptions, procedures followed to evaluate the financial consequences of contract changes are deficient in these respects:

1. Cost calculations are past, rather than future, oriented. Firms assume that the amount of labor used and the mix of rates at which labor was compensated in the past will suffice as guides to the future. They base computations on historical, as opposed to projected, levels of operations.

2. The analytical techniques consider only the direct ramifications of contract changes, and they emphasize the cost, instead of the effect on profits, of such changes. The firms pay insufficient attention to relationships among labor costs, volume, product mix and capital investments, and they disregard their ability to mini-

mize, by modifying previously formulated corporate plans, the financial consequences of increases in compensation.

3. The algorithms employed are sometimes improper. For example, in computing the cost of direct-wage increases, many firms ignore the impact on "roll-up" of changes in benefits negotiated concurrently with changes in wages. Similarly, in estimating outlays that would be necessitated by increases in paid time off, some firms neglect wage premiums that they will be required to pay employees who will have to work overtime in order to maintain production volume at planned levels.

RESPONSIBILITY FOR CONTRACT ANALYSIS AND RELATIONSHIPS AMONG DEPARTMENTS

In most firms, an industrial (or labor) relations department has primary responsibility for all phases of collective bargaining, including financial analysis. In only two companies visited is the finance department in charge of determining the financial consequences of contract changes.

Several of the firms make no use, in contract evaluation, of the analytical skills of either accountants or members of the finance staff, who are more likely than industrial relations personnel to have quantitative backgrounds. In all firms studied, the accounting or finance department supplies information, upon request, to the industrial relations department, but often the data are nothing more than summaries of payroll accounts.

All companies prepare "long range" plans indicating anticipated volume, prices, capital investment and product mix for a period at least as long as that covered by their labor agreements. Yet in some firms such forecasts are never given to the industrial relations department. Persons involved in contract analysis must make their own projections or rely upon those received "informally" from colleagues in other departments. In others, the industrial relations department receives, but does not use, the forecasts. With few exceptions, the firms interviewed use primarily demographic and accounting data, but relatively little financial (internal economic) information. Contract analysts tend, perhaps because of the limited amount of information they receive about the plans of other departments, to disregard the effects of their decisions on other functional areas of the corporation.

By contrast, in two firms which make the most extensive use of financial data, the finance department has primary responsibility for determining the financial consequences of contract changes. These firms give the greatest consideration of any companies studied to the indirect effects of contract changes and compute the cost of changes using projected as well as historical data. Indeed, there is a distinct correlation between the degree of involvement in collective bargaining of departments other than industrial relations and the extent to which the firms take into account information normally found in corporate budgets or internal operating reports. Presumably, firms which are aware of the most probable "true" financial outcomes of alternative proposals are better able than those which are not to make decisions that will lead to realization of collective-bargaining objectives.

THE DISCOUNTED CASH FLOW MODEL

Feasibility

The discounted cash flow model may considerably strengthen the evaluation procedures of many firms. The model fosters consideration of the consequences of contract changes on profits as well as on costs, and it requires that the firm explicitly take into account anticipated, rather than past, corporate performance. In addition, it introduces a new variable, the time value of money, into the analysis.

Few if any firms currently use the discounted cash flow model to evaluate contract proposals. But there is evidence, nonetheless, that it is a feasible technique.

One firm, which participated in the study, currently identifies the critical cash flows associated with contract changes. It gives consideration to modifications in operations that it is likely to make in response to contract changes, and it bases all labor-cost projections on its "estimated planning volume," which indicates, by month, anticipated production volume, product mix and labor requirements. The firm specifically determines the impact of contract revisions on both cash flow and profits. To this firm, use of the discounted cash flow model would necessitate a relatively minor extension of techniques presently employed. The model would require only that the company adjust the estimated cash flows to take into account the time value of money.

Other firms evaluate a few specific contract provisions in the context of overall operations. One firm, in computing the cost of additional holidays, makes allowance for the cost of expanding its plant. Since the company is operating at capacity, it could maintain current production volume only by enlarging its facilities. The firm adds to the direct cost of holiday pay and related benefits the annual cost of the capital required to finance the expansion.

The airline at which interviews were conducted integrates evaluations of contract proposals with those of planned schedule and equipment changes. The wages of flight personnel are dependent upon the types of aircraft flown, so that before they are able to compute the cost of pay increases, analysts must be advised of plans to introduce new equipment. Labor agreements in the airline industry restrict the number of hours that flight personnel are permitted to fly both consecutively and within prescribed time periods. Consequently, changes in restrictions may necessitate changes in flight schedules or increases in the number of pilots and flight attendants employed. Determination of the costs of such changes requires that the plans of the labor relations department be coordinated with those of the operations department.

Such firms demonstrate that it is feasible to integrate decisions involving collective bargaining with those concerned with other corporate activities.

Availability of Data

At every company studied, officials stated that the data required by the discounted cash flow model are currently available within their firms and could be made accessible to the department in charge of contract analysis. Some labor relations officials said that they currently receive the necessary forecasts; others were certain that they would be provided upon their request.

The managers interviewed could think of no accounting records, in addition to those which they presently need, which would have to be maintained specifically to provide data for the discounted cash flow model—although a few pointed out that the accounting records of their firms do not presently furnish them with adequate information with which to evaluate certain contract terms.

The discounted cash flow model requires no special information that well-managed firms do not currently compile. The model is more likely, however, than conventional techniques to reveal inadequacies in information systems presently maintained.

Implementation

To executives unfamiliar with cash discounting procedures, reports in which labor costs are expressed as present values might be confusing. Such confusion might be minimized if, when the discounted cash flow model is first employed, present-value statistics are given only as a supplement to conventional reports. Similarly, it might be helpful if the cost of specific provisions was continued to be expressed in cents per hour, instead of total dollar amounts. The cents-per-hour cost, however, should denote not the average hourly cost as traditionally computed, but rather the net present value of all anticipated changes in cash flow divided by the estimated annual number of productive labor hours during the life of the contract under consideration.

In attempting to determine alternative wage packages that are of equal cost to the firm, but which may meet with varying degrees of acceptance by the union, an executive may find wage tables, such as those described in Chapter V, useful, albeit cumbersome. But the utility of such tables is limited in that they permit users to compare only two types of contract proposals: those in which the increases are front-loaded and those in which they are spread evenly over the life of the contract. Of greater value in implementing the discounted cash flow model would be a computer software package which enables an executive to enter into the computer, through an office terminal, proposals which he is considering and receive in return alternative proposals which would have the same present value.

CONCLUDING COMMENT

The discounted cash flow model can be employed to evaluate the financial consequences both of an entire contract and of specific provisions, as long as both the direct and the indirect changes in cash flow can be identified. In many instances variables such as price, volume, product mix and capital mix would be insensitive to minor changes in specific contract provisions. Increases in prices, for example, may certainly be associated with changes in labor costs. However, prices are also affected by many other factors. Seldom would a firm specifically raise prices in response to, for example, an increase in the number of paid holidays. But if the firm is operating at capacity, it may have to revise its estimates of production volume. The discounted cash flow model enables management to explicitly consider if operational adjustments would, in fact, be expedient.

Officials interviewed reported several reasons why they do not pay particular attention to potential changes in economic variables: projections are unreliable; either total or per-unit labor costs do not vary with output; prices and product mix are insensitive to labor costs; labor costs are but a minor influence on decisions whether to add new facilities. Nevertheless, for many firms, labor compensation is the largest single operating cost. Insofar as any economic variables are affected by costs, they are most certainly affected by changes in labor costs. To be sure, in formulating corporate plans all firms studied forecast increases in labor costs and optimize their operating strategies accordingly. The value of the discounted cash flow model, however, is that it requires the firm, when reviewing proposals for actual wage increases, to compare proposed costs with projected costs and to determine whether adjustments in original corporate plans are both feasible and advisable.

The model enables firms to utilize information which they currently compile and which would be available to them at no additional cost. Even if companies elect not to introduce present values into their evaluations, the analysis that they perform is likely to lead to greater understanding of the effect on profits of contract revisions.

APPENDIX I

Additional Information on Methodology of Study and Outline Followed in Interviews

The interviews at the 11 firms studied were conducted with labor relations, accounting and finance personnel—in all cases with persons who are closely involved in making decisions which relate to contract bargaining. In some companies interviews were conducted with only industrial relations personnel. But in such companies, the officials interviewed indicated that virtually all cost analysis is done within their departments.

The interviews at each firm lasted for three to eight hours. Usually they were conducted in one day; several times, however, return visits were made. The interviews were informal, but generally followed a prepared outline (see below). First, responsibility for collective bargaining and organizational relationships among departments sharing the responsibility were discussed. Then the company's procedures for developing management proposals and evaluating union proposals and the techniques used in analyzing specific contract changes were reviewed. Finally, the discounted cash flow model was presented and the officials were asked to evaluate its utility for their particular firm. In all cases, discussions focused on methodology of analysis rather than on specific cost or revenue figures. In order to obtain cooperation from the officials, they were assured both that their firm would not be identified in this report and that there would be no need for them to disclose confidential cost or revenue data.

Although it was originally intended to study only firms that engage in national as opposed to local or plant bargaining, it quickly became apparent that many major firms do not, in fact, bargain with only a single major union on a national level. However, preliminary investigations did not reveal significant differences in methods used to evaluate contracts between firms that engage in national bargaining and those that engage in local bargaining. Officers of those firms that engage in local bargaining indicated that negotiations with one or two particular locals generally establish a pattern for settlements with other locals, and that when proposals are analyzed in preparation for contract talks with the pattern-establishing union, the firms assume that the major features of the contract will be incorporated into the agreements with other unions as well.

One company studied engages in industry-wide bargaining. The major firms in the industry prepare jointly for bargaining and negotiate together with a single union. The company's ability to influence the final settlement is, therefore, limited. Nevertheless, the company does have to analyze the impact of any proposal on its own profits, and its method of analysis is not substantially different than those of the firms studied that bargain independently.

The following is a general outline of the format of the interviews:

I. Responsibility for Collective Bargaining
   A. Which department has overall responsibility?
   B. Who are the members of the bargaining team?
   C. Which departments supply data to be employed in estimating the financial impact of contract changes?
   D. Which departments analyze such data?
   E. Which officials have authority to approve company proposals or reject union proposals?
   F. Which officials formulate bargaining strategy?

II. Relationships Among Departments
   A. What are the directions of the flows of information among departments?
   B. How do formal channels of communication differ from informal channels?
   C. Which departments initiate requests for information; which departments respond to requests?

III. Development of Company Proposals
   A. What are the major stages in preparation for bargaining? When do they take place?

B. What is the sequence of bargaining decisions (i.e., does the company first determine the total dollar value of its offer and then the components or does it first determine the components and then total dollar value)?

C. What types of data are used in evaluating the financial impact of alternative contract proposals?
   1. What are the sources of such data?
   2. What accounts or records are maintained specifically to supply such data?

D. What quantitative techniques are used to estimate the financial impact of contract changes?

E. How does management identify clauses which are in company interest to change?

F. How does the company rank alternative proposals?

G. Does the firm engage in "mock" bargaining?

IV. Methods Used to Determine the Financial Impact of Contract Changes?

A. How is the financial impact of changes involving the following estimated?
   1. Wage rates (timing of increases)
      a. Measured day work
      b. Incentive rates
      c. Overtime premium
   2. Wage structure
      a. Job classifications
      b. Changes in jobs because of technological improvements
      c. Inequity claims
      d. Automatic increases
      e. Cost-of-living increases
   3. Seniority rules and benefits
      a. Promotions
      b. Transfers
      c. Work assignments
      d. Shift preferences
      e. Overtime distribution
   4. Profit-sharing plans
   5. Work-sharing and layoff plans
      a. Bumping provisions
      b. SUB
   6. Work scheduling
      a. Definition of workweek
      b. Shift premiums
      c. Penalty payments

    7. Production standards
    8. Pension plans
    9. Health and welfare plans
  10. Income security and severance pay plans
  11. Contract administration
     a. Arbitration of grievances
     b. Time off for union activities
  12. Training and apprenticeship programs
  13. Miscellaneous contract provisions
     a. Rest periods
     b. Vacations
     c. Improved facilities
     d. Medical exams
     e. Holidays

B. What consideration is given to the relationships among labor costs and the following variables? How are the following variables estimated?
  1. Sales and prices
  2. Nonlabor costs
  3. Labor-related costs
  4. Product mix
  5. Capital investment
  6. "Spillover"

V. Management's Assessment of the Discounted Cash Flow Model
A. What data, in addition to those currently being collected, would management require if it were to use the discounted cash flow model; are such data readily available?
B. What changes in organizational relationships and accounting systems would be necessitated by a decision to use the discounted cash flow model?
C. What difficulties would management foresee in making the estimates required by the discounted cash flow model?
D. What difficulties would management foresee in determining the number of years for which a given contract change will affect the company's operations?

VI. Miscellaneous
A. What type of post-contract analysis is made?
B. What are some major errors that the firm has made that were due to faulty analysis?

Equations of Discounted Cash Flow Model

The formulas for computing the present value of a front-loaded contract, a spread contract, or any contract with a uniform pattern of first-contract wage increases can be developed from the basic present value equation:

(6-1) $$PV = F(1+r)^{-n}$$

where

PV = present value of a given sum
F = equivalent future value n periods hence
r = discount rate

The present value per $1.00 of wages of a single front-loaded contract is the summation, for the number of years of the contract, of $(1+r)^{-n}$ times the wage rate, which remains constant over the life of the contract. Thus (with slightly different notation):

(6-2) $$PV = (1+G)\,[(1+r)^{-1} + (1+r)^{-2} + \ldots (1+r)^{-L}]$$

where

PV = present value per $1 of wages
L = length in years of the contract
r = an appropriate discount rate
G = percentage by which wages have increased over those prescribed in the prior contract.

The factor $(1+G)$ has been substituted in equation 6-2 for F to take into account the increase over the wage rate, which is assumed to be $1, of the expiring contract. Hence, $(1+G)$ denotes the wage proposed for the first contract.

The present value of a front-loaded contract evaluated over more than one contract period is the sum of the present values of the several single contracts, or:

$$PV = \sum_{j=1}^{j=N/L} (1+G)^j \left[(1+r)^{-(i-L+1)} + (1+r)^{-(i-L+2)} \dots (1+r)^{-(i-L+L)}\right]$$

where

    PV = present value of \$1 of wages
    L = length of each contract
    j = contract under consideration
    i = jL
    N = perspective of management in total number of years
    r = an appropriate discount rate
    G = percentage by which wages will increase each contract.

The factor $(1+G)^j$ represents the wage rate during each contract under consideration. The formula can be further simplified to:

(6-3)

$$PV = \sum_{j=1}^{j=N/L} (1+G)^j \left[\frac{(1+r)^{-(i-L)} - (1+r)^{-i}}{r}\right]$$

To determine the present value of a contract in which the increase is spread over the life of the contract, minor modification of the equation is required. In computing the present value of a front-loaded contract, it is assumed that wages will increase at a constant rate of growth per contract. In computing the present value of a spread contract it is taken for granted that wages will increase by the same rate of growth, but as explained earlier, it is also assumed that the firm will pay an additional premium that will be permanently incorporated into the wage structure. Thus, the total increase during the first contract will be equal to the previous wage times the growth rate, plus the premium. The increase in each year of the contract will be equal to the previous wage times the growth rate, plus the premium, divided by the number of years in the contract. And the wages in each year of the contract will equal the initial wage plus the appropriate number of increases.

The formula for computing the present value per \$1 of the first contract of the spread alternative would therefore be:

(6-4)

$$PV = \sum_{n=1}^{n=L} 1 + n[\frac{G+P}{L}] (1+r)^{-n}$$

where, in addition to the notation already indicated:

n = year under consideration

P = the premium, or difference between the total wage increase during the first contract, and the estimated rate of growth times the ending wage rate under the previous contract.

Equation 6-4 is the equivalent for the spread alternative of equation 6-2, the present value of the initial front-loaded contract. The formula for computing the present value of subsequent contracts after the first remains essentially the same as that for front-loaded contracts with the exception that recognition must be given to the premium, which is incorporated into the wage structure. Hence, an additional "P" is added to the formula:

(6-5)

$$PV = \sum_{j=2}^{j=N/L} \{(1+G)^j + P\}[\frac{(1+r)^{-(i-L)} - (1+r)^{-i}}{r}]$$

Combined, the overall formula is:

(6-6)

$$PV = \sum_{n=1}^{n=L} 1 + n[\frac{G+P}{L}] (1+r)^{-n} +$$

$$\sum_{j=2}^{j=N/L} \{(1+G)^j + P\}[\frac{(1+r)^{-(i-L)} - (1+r)^{-i}}{r}]$$

With the additional modifications, the formula can be adapted to permit the computation of the present value of any pattern of wage increases. The increases need not be either front-loaded or spread evenly over the life of the contract. If the assumptions regarding future growth of wages are maintained, the formula for the present value of

wages to be paid after the expiration of the first contract is identical
to that for the years subsequent to the expiration of the spread contract
(equation 6-5):

$$\sum_{j=2}^{j=N/L} \{(1+G)^j+P\}[\frac{(1+r)^{-(i-L)} - (1+r)^{-i}}{r}]$$

As before, "P," the premium, represents the difference between the
actual wage at the end of the first contract and the wage that would
have been in effect had wages increased by the estimated per contract
rate of growth (e.g., the increase had been front-loaded). The present
value of wages paid during the first contract would be the sum of the
present values of the wages during each of the years of the contract—
the sum of $(1+r)^{-n}$ times the wages paid in each of the years:

$$PV = w_1(1+r)^{-1} + w_2(1+r)^{-2} + \ldots w_L(1+r)^{-L}$$

where $w_n =$ the wage rate in each year of the first contract. And
combined:

(6-7)

$$PV = w_1(1+r)^{-1} + w_2(1+r)^{-2} + \ldots w_L(1+r)^{-L} +$$

$$\sum_{j=2}^{j=N/L} \{(1+G)^j+P\}[\frac{(1+r)^{-(i-L)} - (1+r)^{-i}}{r}]$$

The wage increases proposed by management, it should be emphasized, may be independent of management's estimate of the "long run"
rate of growth of wages. The total percentage increase proposed for
the first contract may be greater or less than the estimated growth percentage. Management, for example, may propose a first-contract increase
of 25 percent, even though it expects wages to increase by only 20
percent per contract over the "long run."

Equations 6-6 and 6-7, those for computing the present value of
a spread contract and a contract where first-contract increases do not
follow an established pattern, automatically take into account differences
between the percentage increase of wages in the first contract and those
in subsequent contracts. Equation 6-3, that for computing the present
value of a front-loaded contract, however, does not. Thus, where management proposes an initial percentage increase greater or less than
the long-run percentage, it is necessary to incorporate into the equation

provision for a premium, the difference between the first-contract wage actually proposed and the wage that would have been proposed had the long-run growth percentage been applicable to the first contract.

The wage rate during each year of the first contract (assuming a previous wage of $1) would equal:

$$1 + G + P$$

and the present value of such wages would be:

$$\sum_{n=1}^{n=L} (1+G+P)(1+r)^{-n}$$

That of subsequent contracts will be the same as previously indicated, except for the addition of P, the premium:

$$\sum_{j=2}^{j=N/L} \{(1+G)^J+P\}[\frac{(1+r)^{-(i-L)} - (1+r)^{-i}}{r}]$$

Combined, therefore, the formula for computing the present value of a front-loaded contract when the percentage increase during the first contract is different from that anticipated for the long run is:

(6-3a)

$$\sum_{n=1}^{n=L} (1+G+P)(1+r)^{-n} +$$

$$\sum_{j=2}^{j=N/L} \{(1+G)^J+P\}[\frac{(1+r)^{-(i-L)} - (1+r)^{-i}}{r}]$$

The example used previously in the text can serve to demonstrate the use of the present value equations. Management has decided that it can "afford" increases of $.15 the first year of a three-year contract, $.10 the second year and $.05 the third year. The current wage is $1, the perspective of management is four contracts (12 years), the appropriate discount rate is 18 percent, and management anticipates that over the next several years wage rates will rise at a per-contract rate of 20 percent. The present value of the offer can be computed, using equation 6-7, to be $7.24:

$$PV = 1.15(1+.18)^{-1} + 1.25(1+.18)^{-2} + 1.30(1+.18)^{-3} +$$

$$\sum_{j=2}^{j=4} \{(1+.20)^j + .10\}[\frac{(1+.18)^{-(i-3)} - (1+.18)^{-i}}{.18}] = 7.2393$$

Management can now use the equations for the present value of a front-loaded contract (6-3a) and for a spread contract (6-6) to develop alternative offers that will have the same present value of $7.24.

By setting equation 6-3a equal to $7.24 and solving for P, the required premium can be calculated to be $.066:

$$7.2393 = \sum_{n=1}^{n=3} (1+.20+P)(1+.18)^{-n} +$$

$$\sum_{j=2}^{j=4} \{(1+.18)^j + P\}[\frac{(1+.18)^{-(i-3)} - (1+.18)^{-i}}{.18}]$$

If P is equal to $.066, then the total first-contract increase must be $.20 plus $.066 or $.266, and the equivalent front-loaded wage would, therefore, be $1.266. The comparable spread increase can be determined by setting 6-6 equal to $7.24 and again solving for P, the premium:

$$7.2393 = \sum_{n=1}^{n=3} 1 + n[\frac{.20 + P}{3}](1 + .18)^{-n} +$$

$$\sum_{j=2}^{j=4} (1+.20)^j + P[\frac{(1+.18)^{-(i-3)} - (1+.18)^{-i}}{.18}]$$

Therefore,

P = .120.

Since the premium equals $.12, the total increase at the expiration of the first contract must equal $.12 plus $.20 (the increase based on the long-run rate of growth) or $.32. Hence, the annual increases are $.32 divided by 3, the length of the contract, or $.107 and the first contract wages would be $1.107, $1.214 and $1.320.

Topical Index